THOMAS OTWAY

Venice Preserved

Edited by

MALCOLM KELSALL

EDWARD ARNOLD

Cloth edition: SBN 7131 5470 5
Paper edition: SBN 7131 5471 3

Printed in Great Britain by
William Clowes and Sons, Limited, London and Beccles

Regents Restoration Drama Series

The Regents Restoration Drama Series provides soundly edited texts, in modern spelling, of the more significant plays of the late seventeenth and early eighteenth centuries. The word "Restoration" is here used ambiguously and must be explained. If to the historian it refers to the period between 1660 and 1685 (or 1688), it has long been used by the student of drama in default of a more precise word to refer to plays belonging to the dramatic tradition established in the 1660's, weakening after 1700, and displaced in the 1730's. It is in this extended sense—imprecise though justified by academic custom—that the word is used in this series, which includes plays first produced between 1660 and 1737. Although these limiting dates are determined by political events, the return of Charles II (and the removal of prohibitions against operation of theaters) and the passage of Walpole's Stage Licensing Act, they enclose a period of dramatic history having a coherence of its own in the establishment, development, and disintegration of a tradition.

Some eighteen editions having appeared as this volume goes to press, the series has reached over a third of its anticipated range of between forty and fifty volumes. The volumes will continue to be published for a number of years, at the rate of three or more annually. From the beginning the editors have planned the series with attention to the projected dimensions of the completed whole, a representative collection of Restoration drama providing a record of artistic achievement and providing also a record of the deepest concerns of three generations of Englishmen. And thus it contains deservedly famous plays—*The Country Wife*, *The Man of Mode*, and *The Way of the World*—and also significant but little known plays, *The Virtuoso*, for example, and *City Politiques*, the former a satirical review of scientific investigation in the early years of the Royal Society, the latter an equally satirical review of politics at the time of the Popish Plot. If the volumes of famous plays finally achieve the larger circulation, the other volumes may conceivably have the greater utility, in making available texts otherwise difficult of access with the editorial apparatus needed to make them intelligible.

The editors have had the instructive example of the parallel and senior project, the Regents Renaissance Drama Series; they have in fact used the editorial policies developed for the earlier plays as their own, modifying them as appropriate for the later period and as the experience of successive editions suggested. The introductions to the separate Restoration plays differ considerably in their nature. Although a uniform body of relevant information is presented in each of them, no attempt has been made to impose a pattern of interpretation. Emphasis in the introductions has necessarily varied with the nature of the plays and inevitably—we think desirably—with the special interests and aptitudes of the different editors.

Each text in the series is based on a fresh collation of the seventeenth- and eighteenth-century editions that might be presumed to have authority. The textual notes, which appear above the rule at the bottom of each page, record all substantive departures from the edition used as the copy-text. Variant substantive readings among contemporary editions are listed there as well. Editions later than the eighteenth century are referred to in the textual notes only when an emendation originating in some one of them is received into the text. Variants of accidentals (spelling, punctuation, capitalization) are not recorded in the notes. Contracted forms of characters' names are silently expanded in speech prefixes and stage directions and, in the case of speech prefixes, are regularized. Additions to the stage directions of the copy-text are enclosed in brackets.

Spelling has been modernized along consciously conservative lines, but within the limits of a modernized text the linguistic quality of the original has been carefully preserved. Contracted preterites have regularly been expanded. Punctuation has been brought into accord with modern practices. The objective has been to achieve a balance between the pointing of the old editions and a system of punctuation which, without overloading the text with exclamation marks, semicolons, and dashes, will make the often loosely flowing verse and prose of the original syntactically intelligible to the modern reader. Dashes are regularly used only to indicate interrupted speeches, or shifts of address within a single speech.

Explanatory notes, chiefly concerned with glossing obsolete words and phrases, are printed below the textual notes at the bottom of each page. References to stage directions in the notes follow the admirable system of the Revels editions, whereby stage directions are keyed, decimally, to the line of the text before or after which they occur.

REGENTS RESTORATION DRAMA SERIES

General Editor: John Loftis

VENICE PRESERVED

Thus, a note on 0.2 has reference to the second line of the stage direction at the beginning of the scene in question. A note on 115.1 has reference to the first line of the stage direction following line 115 of the text of the relevant scene. Speech prefixes, and any stage directions attached to them, are keyed to the first line of accompanying dialogue.

JOHN LOFTIS

August, 1968
Stanford University

Contents

List of Abbreviations

F1   First separate edition of prologue and epilogue (printed for A. Green), 1682

F2   Second separate edition of prologue and epilogue (printed for A. Banks), 1682

G   *The Works of Thomas Otway*, ed. J. C. Ghosh. Oxford, 1932.

Q1   First Quarto, 1682

Q2   Second Quarto, 1696

Q3   Third Quarto, 1704

S.D.   stage direction

W   *The Works of Mr. Thomas Otway.* London, 1712.

Introduction

The only edition of *Venice Preserved* to appear in Otway's lifetime
was the quarto of 1682 printed for Joseph Hindmarsh and recorded in
The Term Catalogues for Easter (May) of that year. This is the basis of
the present edition. The copy-text is from the Bodleian Library,
Oxford (Mal. B. 272). This has been collated with the "variant"
first quarto in Bodley (in which the final "e" is omitted from "theatre"
on the title page), but no substantive variants have been found. There
were two issues of a second edition in 1696, one printed for R.
Bentley and James Knapton, the other for Knapton alone, and a
third edition in 1704. These have been collated with the first quarto,
as has also the text printed by Tonson in the collected edition of
Otway's *Works*, 1712. The first quarto was carelessly set; the second
follows the first closely but corrects numerous errors; the third was
set from the second but introduces several unnecessary emendations;
and the text in the *Works* was derived from the third quarto. In the
present edition the obvious misprints in the first quarto have been
silently corrected. Variants from the later editions accepted into the
present text, and a few viable alternative readings, are recorded in the
textual apparatus.

Venice Preserved, or, a Plot Discovered was first performed by the
Duke's Company at Dorset Garden on February 9, 1682.[1] The
ostensible cause of the production was political. As the subtitle indi-
cates, Otway was exploiting for literary ends the furore caused by the
Popish Plot, and the play was offered by the Company to celebrate
the fall of Shaftesbury and the collapse of the Whigs' maneuvers to
exclude the Duke of York from the succession.[2] Almost two years

[1] The date is according to the folio half sheet on which the prologue and
epilogue first appeared.

[2] For an elaborate hypothesis relating the composition of *Venice Preserved*
to contemporary events see Aline Mackenzie, "*Venice Preserv'd* Reconsid-
ered," *Tulane Studies in English*, I (1949), 81–118. It is argued that the play
was begun shortly after September, 1678, and rewritten to introduce
Antonio after the fall of Shaftesbury in 1681.

separate the performance from the production of Otway's previous play, *The Soldier's Fortune* (March, 1680). In the meantime Charles II, secured by a French subsidy, had dissolved the Oxford Parliament (March, 1681), and although the move to indict Shaftesbury for high treason had recently failed (November, 1681), at the end of 1682 he fled the country.

Otway had already dedicated *Don Carlos* (1676) to the Duke of York, and *The Orphan* (1680) to the Duchess. The dedication now of *Venice Preserved* to Charles' French mistress, Louise Renée de Kérouaille, Duchess of Portsmouth, and the prologue and epilogue which bait the Whigs, reaffirmed his allegiance. Otway's major political success, however, was in the "Nicky Nacky" scenes,[3] for Antonio was immediately recognised as a portrait of Anthony Ashley Cooper.[4] This caricature of Shaftesbury (who was, like Antonio, supposedly sixty-one years old)[5] in its emphasis upon his lewdness, his physical disability, and his oratorical presumption, clearly resembles Dryden's portrait of the Whig leader in *Absalom and Achitophel* and *The Medal*. To the perverted Senator was added the corrupt conspirator, for Renault is Shaftesbury in another guise. Otway had his reward. The third night of the play, for the author's benefit, was attended by the king. The Duke of York, returned from diplomatic exile in Scotland, attended a performance on April 21 celebrated by a special prologue by Dryden and a new epilogue by Otway. On May 31 the Duchess visited the theater. Again Dryden wrote a prologue and Otway an epilogue.

Much of this political satire can be seen as extraneous to the main action of the play. The Nicky Nacky scenes were omitted some years before 1718.[6] Whether this was a result of a change in taste or politics is not certain, but the action of *Venice Preserved* is inconsistent as

[3] See, for instance, Mrs. Aphra Behn's "The Cabal at Nickey Nackeys," in *Poems Upon Several Occasions* (1684), p. 125. Roswell G. Ham, "Additional Material for a Life of Otway," *Notes and Queries*, CL (1926), 75–77, quotes a Whig satire in the Harleian MSS (7319, p. 225) in which an Ensign of the Guards declares: "He liked the scene of *Nicky Nacky*, more / Than all that *Shadwell* ever writ before."

[4] For a detailed examination of the political allusions in the play see John Robert Moore, "Contemporary Satire in Otway's *Venice Preserved*," *PMLA*, XLIII (1928), 166–181.

[5] Otway miscalculated. Shaftesbury was not sixty-one until July 22, 1682.

[6] See Charles Gildon, *The Complete Art of Poetry* (1718), I, 237.

political allegory.[7] Both the Senate and the conspirators are corrupt, and if either may stand for the Whigs, both can scarcely do so. Moreover, although Tory propaganda required that the Popish Plot should be shown as a Whig fabrication, in the play there is no doubt as to the existence of a major conspiracy motivated for reasons with which the audience may sympathize. Finally, the three major characters, Belvidera, Jaffeir, and Pierre, have no counterparts in contemporary history. The main action of the play turns upon love and friendship, not upon political principles. Nonetheless, *Venice Preserved* would not be as it is without the background of the Popish Plot. The principal actors are destroyed between the upper and nether millstones of a wicked Senate (the Whig Parliament) and an evil conspiracy. Without Antonio/Shaftesbury, the corruption of the Senate would not be plain; without Renault, Antonio's alter ego, the evil nature of the plot would be obscured.

In a larger sense, also, the corruption, the betrayals and the divided loyalties of the action reflect only too well the dilemmas of 1678–1682. Although it has become commonplace to say that the roots of Otway's tragedies lie in Jacobean drama,[8] he had no need to turn back to the Italy of lurid Jacobean imagination in shaping *Venice Preserved*. The blend of high ideals and bloody deeds which confuses the reader's loyalties during the action, the story of weak people trapped in a corrupt society, the whole explosive emotional atmosphere, even the involvement of sexual desires and political motive, may be easily paralleled in general terms in the history of the times. It is indicative of Otway's dilemma that he nowhere mentions Edward Coleman, the traitor and former secretary of the Duke of

[7] An attempt to read the play as a coherent allegory is made by Zera S. Fink, *The Classical Republicans* (Evanston, Illinois, 1945), pp. 144–148. It is suggested that "Venice . . . is a hostile, Tory representation, not of the England that the Whigs were accused of conspiring against, but of what is taken as the Whig ideal of a Venetian state." But Fink admits "this interpretation makes the conspirators of the play stand in the allegory for the system which they were plotting to overthrow."

[8] H. Taine, *Histoire de la Littérature Anglaise* (8th. edn., Paris, 1892), III, 209, made the parallel with characteristic force. William H. McBurney, "Otway's Tragic Muse Debauched: Sensuality in *Venice Preserv'd*," *Journal of English and Germanic Philology*, LVIII (1959), 380–399, calls the play "a somber indictment of the late Restoration world . . . a dark satiric tragedy worthy of the Jacobean dramatists." See also Roswell Gray Ham, *Otway and Lee* (New Haven, 1931), p. 184.

York, and despite his jibes in the prologue at the story of the murder of Edmund Berry Godfrey, if the claim of Tory propaganda that Godfrey committed suicide was untrue, then it is extremely probable that he was murdered for political motives. The Court dared not take legal measures against Oates until 1684. The Duchess of Portsmouth, running with both sides, had encouraged her son, Charles Lennox (1672–1723), to strike the bar sinister from his coat of arms as the more famous royal bastard, the Duke of Monmouth, had done, and a substantial bribe had carried her for a time to the side of the Whigs. Otway can have known nothing of Charles' own maneuvers to clear the way for the establishment of absolute monarchy by Catholic arms, but enough was public, and there were suspicions of worse, to confuse even the most loyal Tory.

Hence the coloring of cynicism in *Venice Preserved*. It is not entirely surprising that Otway did not make his way in the world when (albeit in the words of the villainous Renault) he described, in transparent allegory, the condition of the state thus:

> The public stock's a beggar; one Venetian
> Trusts not another. Look into their stores
> Of general safety: empty magazines,
> A tattered fleet, a murmuring unpaid army,
> Bankrupt nobility, a harassed commonalty,
> A factious, giddy, and divided Senate
> Is all the strength of Venice.   (II.iii.69–75)

Even the title of the play is ambiguous, for it is part of the irony of the work that Venice was the most famous *republic* in Europe, and as such, a well-known political model for the Whig extremists.[9] The Duke of York had already warned Charles that the policies of the Whigs would make the king less than the Doge of Venice.[10] Is Venice worth preserving? Who are its true preservers? Pierre sees himself as Marcus Brutus, the savior of the state from would-be monarchical tyranny, but Renault models himself on Catiline, traditionally a type of the violent and wicked conspirator. *Venice Preserved* read as a Tory political allegory is not consistent; as a mirror of the times it reflects the age only too well.

Like Nathaniel Lee in *Lucius Junius Brutus* (1680) and Joseph Addison in *Cato* (1713), Otway makes his comment on contemporary

9 See Zera S. Fink, *The Classical Republicans*.
10 John Pollock, *The Popish Plot* (London, 1903), p. 218.

affairs by the use of parallel history. The basis of the story, and much of the interpretation of events, was drawn from *La Conjuration des Espagnols contre la République de Venise* (1674), an account of an abortive insurrection in 1618 by the philosophical (and inventive) French historian César Vischard, l'abbé de Saint-Réal. It was translated into English as *A Conspiracy of the Spaniards Against the State of Venice* (published in 1675). There was a second edition in 1679, probably occasioned by the Popish Plot. Otway used the translation.[11] Both in France and England the work has often been reprinted.

The story told by Saint-Réal has as its background the struggle of Venice against the power of Rome, and, more immediately, the defense of the republic against the intrigues of the Spanish Ambassador, Don Alphonso de la Cueva, Marquis of Bedamar (Otway's Bedamore). Hence the topical appeal for an English audience. The plot in the French narration was no mere informer's fabrication. The mercenary army in Venice had been corrupted; a mutiny in the fleet had been planned; a Spanish fleet under the Viceroy of Naples waited only for the insurrection to descend on the Venetians.

Although Bedamar was the prime mover in Saint-Réal's narration, both Pierre and Renault feature largely also in the historical plot. Renault, described as "an ancient French gentleman," one, who although he "preferred virtue to riches, howbeit could sacrifice his virtue to his ambition,"[12] had the task of bribing the Venetian mercenaries to join the insurrection. The speech in which he gave final instructions to the conspirators was closely followed by Otway. To Pierre, a corsair, but "a man whose manners had taken no impression from the barbarity of that course of life," fell the task of destroying the Venetian fleet. Both Pierre and Renault, it is curious to observe, shared as their mistress the noble Greek courtesan who becomes in Otway the rather less noble Aquilina. It was at her house that the conspirators chose to meet as a place of common resort.

Saint-Réal tells that the conspiracy was betrayed at the last moment by Anthony "Jaffier", one of Pierre's "most intimate friends," whom Pierre claimed to be "one of the bravest men living." Jaffeir, torn between his loyalty to his friends and the "funest image" of pillaged and burning Venice, was unable to conceal his distraction of mind from the eyes of Renault, who, accordingly, sought to have him

[11] See Alfred Johnson, *Lafosse, Otway, Saint-Réal* . . . (Paris, 1901), pp. 96–100.

[12] See the opening of II, iii.

killed. Only the intervention of Pierre saved his life, and hence, in both source and play, it is the love of Pierre for his friend that precipitates disaster. Otway, however, supplies a new motivation for Jaffeir. The unfortunate Belvidera is nowhere to be found in the original. Political idealism or lust for plunder provide the driving force for Saint-Réal's characters; love and sexual desire are the ostensible forces in Otway's. Thus, in the climactic scenes, Otway moves away from his source. The Senate's oath to Jaffeir, and their subsequent treachery (on the excuse that information has come from elsewhere) belong to the original, but Pierre is stabbed on shipboard, Jaffeir drowned on the Senate's orders. The macabre theatrical climax of love, murder, suicide, and madness in *Venice Preserved* was inspired rather by Webster.

It was more than the story, however, which attracted Otway to Saint-Réal. The philosophical historian had a clear insight into the passions and distraction of spirit which conspiracy evokes. Prudence and judgment are rare in conspirators, he observed. "Panic fear" and its converse, the infirmity of extravagant friendship, too great a "subjection to their passions"—these are the qualities he analysed, nowhere more clearly than in Jaffeir: "But to betray all his friends, and such friends! So brave! So prudent! So singular in the respective talents wherein they excelled!" "Shall he eclipse the glory of reaping the maturest fruit of the most exalted revolution that hath been ever conceived by the spirit of Man?" On which Saint-Réal commented: "Heaven would not abandon the work of twelve ages, and of so many able masters to the fury of a courtesan, and a troop of desperate men."

Just as in Otway, so in Saint-Réal, therefore, the reader is confused where to place his sympathies. The mixed motives of the conspiracy, the divided loyalties of Jaffeir, the inextricable inter-relation of personal emotion and political motive, even the uncertain well-being of the state itself, were clearly revealed in Saint-Réal's narrative. It was the faction within the Senate, the discontent of an oppressed people, the uncertain loyalty of the army, and the veniality of the nobility which encouraged Bedamar in his plot, but there is no indication that revolution would have meant reform. There is a resourceful vigor and intrepidity in the conspirators which is admirable, but it was to Saint-Réal an additional source of "horror" that one should find among them "the most excellent qualities employed to an end the most detestable." Otway, in searching for a parallel in history to his own times, had come upon a tragic dilemma. In *Venice Preserved* the lesson of history is that even the best men are wrong, all shall suffer, and there is nothing for our comfort.

It is this grounding of the story in the truths of political action that is one of the main strengths of Otway's play. But *Venice Preserved* is also the most strikingly "theatrical"—in the praiseworthy sense of the word—of Otway's works. For more than a century it held a place on the London stage "next to Shakespeare,"[13] and was still regularly performed well into the nineteenth century.[14] It continued to succeed in the theater long after the political causes which engendered it had been in the main forgotten, because it provided a magnificent vehicle for the performer. Every great actor and actress from Betterton and Mrs. Barry down to Mrs. Siddons and the Kembles appeared in the leading roles, and there is ample testimony of the play's power. Fanny Kemble's report that she was so carried away by acting Belvidera that she had to be restrained from rushing shrieking from the theater, may be attributed to girlish emotionalism,[15] but such hardened performers as Mrs. Siddons and John Kemble are reported to have been overcome by their parts.[16] Even Addison, who was no admirer of stage effects, admitted the theatrical power of the drama. The tolling of the bell which announces the execution of Pierre, he observed in *The Spectator*, No. 44, "Makes the hearts of the whole audience quake; and conveys a stronger terror to the mind than it is possible for words to do." Mrs. Siddons reduced her audience to tears by Belvidera's mere "Remember twelve," and her scream in the mad scene was still remembered more than a quarter of a century later by Archibald Alison.[17] Miss O'Neill's death scene was even interrupted by the pit rising to their feet applauding and waving their hats, and Edmund Kean, who was not entirely successful in the role of Jaffeir, in "his throwing down the dagger," it is reported "had the effect of electrifying the audience."[18]

13 Oliver Goldsmith, *The Bee*, No. 8. For a full stage history of the play see Aline Mackenzie Taylor, *Next to Shakespeare. Otway's "Venice Preserv'd" and "The Orphan" and their History on the London Stage* (Durham, N. C., 1950), on which I have drawn extensively.

14 The last performances of the play in repertory cited by Taylor are at Covent Garden, December 7, 1838; Drury Lane, April 28, 1842; Sadler's Wells, December 26, 1856.

15 *Records of a Girlhood* (London, 1879), II, 86–87.

16 Cited by Taylor (see note 13), p. 198.

17 *The Dublin Magazine* (1846), p. 531.

18 *The Drama: or the Theatrical Pocket Magazine*, IV (July, 1823), 398.

Nothing more clearly illustrates the nature of Otway's theater and the necessity of reading his text with the mind of an actor than this famous by-play with the dagger, which the stage directions leave open in large measure to the performer. The weapon first becomes prominent when given with Belvidera to the conspirators by Jaffeir in a histrionic gesture. How histrionic the gesture is remains an open question. Heroic convention may have demanded that Jaffeir's pledge be taken seriously. It is not without significance, however, that it is received in almost total silence by the conspirators. Possibly it is with this same dagger that Renault shortly after threatens to kill not Belvidera, but *Jaffeir*. If this is so, the display of the weapon already serves an ironic purpose. The dagger passes thence to Pierre, who in contempt returns it to Jaffeir, after the betrayal. It is now a sign of Jaffeir's worthless honor, and the more he "fumbles" with the dagger before Belvidera, the more this instrument of violence and covert destruction becomes a symbol of the inanity of his words and deeds. It is the final irony that with this same dagger Jaffeir kills Pierre to save him from a more ignoble fate, and then stabbing himself, says to the Officer:

> Sir, I have a wife, bear this in safety to her,
> A token that with my dying breath I blessed her,
> And the dear little infant left behind me.
> I am sick—I'm quiet—.   (V.iii.106–109)

The token is the bloody dagger. If the Officer, when he draws Priuli aside, takes his cue from "stabbed Pierre" and produces the dagger, then at the same moment the ghosts rise, and Belvidera raving dies. The history of the play is that of such dramatic coups. By leaving out the Antonio scenes, however, the eighteenth century omitted one further highly disturbing episode, again involving a dagger: that in which Aquilina threatens Antonio with death, and, unlike Jaffeir with Belvidera, means what she says. Again the action possesses thematic significance. It is another reflection on Jaffeir's ineptitude, for whereas he eventually gives way to his wife, in this scene the woman dominates the man. But, typically, Aquilina's efforts, like those of every other character, come to nothing. Pierre dies, and Antonio lives.

It is not only to the "business," however, that *Venice Preserved* owed its success. Nothing is more striking in the stage history than the variety of interpretation given to the principal parts. Pierre made sense played as an idealist (by Quin), or as a Machiavellian figure during the play's decline. Garrick surprised his audience by portraying the poverty-stricken Jaffeir, not in the traditional dowdy costume, but as a splendid, almost heroic figure. Belvidera might be both gentle and languishing, and a woman of intelligence and strength. The point was well put by the *Athenaeum* in a (hostile) review December 16, 1829: "The author leaves an open field to the performer, not divided by any previous landmarks of the poet's possession, nor dignified by any trophies of his victory." It is perhaps this very openness of interpretation, however, which places Otway in the ambience of Shakespeare. The naturalness which Dryden found in Otway lies in his power to suggest rather than to analyse, to create characters on the stage that move by inner compulsions which an actor may reveal, but which formal analysis in the study may miss behind the superficial facade of eloquence.

Sir Henry Irving, who admired *Venice Preserved* sufficiently to wish to revive it, almost certainly found something of this. Walter Herries Pollock recorded that when Irving recited from the text he "read more into it, in a double sense, than one might perceive in quiet perusal." [19] There surge up through Otway's characters forces and passions which they can neither understand nor control. It is this which led Byron to admire Otway, for Otway is Byronic. His characters throw their roots down to the darkest places of the psyche. When Byron rounded on Belvidera as "that maudlin bitch of chaste lewdness and blubbering curiosity . . . whom I utterly despise, abhor, and detest," [20] though the violence of his expression may be provoked by memories of Lady Byron, he lays open something which the whole tormented love relationship of Jaffeir and Belvidera constantly suggests: the hate, even the masochism, latent in love as violent as theirs.

JAFFEIR.
  No. Do not swear. I would not violate
  Thy tender nature with so rude a bond.
  But as thou hop'st to see me live my days,
  And love thee long, lock this within thy breast;
  I've bound myself by all the strictest sacraments,
  Divine and human—
BELVIDERA.   Speak!—
JAFFEIR.   To kill thy father—

19 *Impressions of Henry Irving* (New York, 1908), p. 135.
20 Letter to John Murray, April 2, 1817.

BELVIDERA.

　My father!

JAFFEIR.

　Nay, the throats of the whole Senate
　Shall bleed, my Belvidera . . .
　. . . whilst thou, far off in safety
　Smiling, shalt see the wonders of our daring,
　And when night comes, with praise and love receive me.

BELVIDERA. Oh!

JAFFEIR.　　　Have a care, and shrink not even in thought!
　For if thou dost—

BELVIDERA.　　　　I know it, thou wilt kill me.
　Do, strike thy sword into this bosom. . . .

　　　　　　　　　　　　　　　　　(III.ii.134–152)

　　The scenes in which Jaffeir receives the news of Renault's attempted rape and recounts it to Pierre show a similar morbid violence. When one restores the Antonio scenes the play becomes more disturbing still. If the dagger scene between Aquilina and Antonio is a parody of that between Jaffeir and Belvidera, are not Antonio's sexual perversions, his subservience to Aquilina, his masochism, all too close to being a gross reflection of the latent tensions between Jaffeir and Belvidera? Even Pierre seems to sense the derangement in the relation of husband and wife. When he gives Jaffeir money in their meeting on the Rialto, his comment is "Here's something to buy pins; / Marriage is chargeable" (II.ii.33–34). Pin-money is more usually given to the wife, not to the husband. Jaffeir, however, is not merely uxorious. There is "pleasure" in the "pain" in which he recounts the ruin that is coming upon himself and his wife. Although his early speeches are open to the interpretation that it is Otway, not Jaffeir, who is wallowing in horrors, nonetheless, in the scene following the conviction of Pierre, Jaffeir's masochism is clearly revealed:

　　　Tread on me, buffet me, heap wrongs on wrongs
　　　On my poor head; I'll bear it all with patience. . . .
　　　Lie at thy feet and kiss 'em though they spurn me. . . .
　　　　　　　　　　　　　　　　　(IV.ii.232–235)

It is thus that he begs forgiveness of Pierre. It is scarcely surprising that Pierre struck him, for he has lost his virtue, his manliness. He is also not far removed from Antonio—"Spit in my face, prithee,"

"Do kick, kick on." How far Otway intended the parallel it is difficult to determine, but some sort of ironic connection between the two characters is at least latent in the action. There is in the relation between them even an element of (unintentional?) black comedy.[21] Why else should Otway provide that Antonio shall remain on stage shamming dead during the last interview between Jaffeir and Belvidera? Antonio is in the play not merely to satirise Shaftesbury. All the evil and all the stupidity in the action are embodied in him.

Finally, in the dénouement of Jaffeir's tragedy, we observe, in Taine's phrase, "l'étrange craquement de la machine qui se démonte." Love and hate, desire to salve his honor and his manhood, yet his dominance by feminine principle, tear him to pieces:

> ... Murder! Perjured Senate!
> Murder—Oh!—Hark thee, traitress, thou hast done this,
> Thanks to thy tears and false persuading love.
> How her eyes speak! Oh thou bewitching creature!
> Madness cannot hurt thee. Come, thou little trembler,
> Creep, even into my heart. ...   (IV.ii.387–392)

If it can be admitted that the ending of the marriage of Jaffeir and Belvidera in self-destruction and madness is implicit from the beginning—she is over-possessive even to the end: "Oh now how I'll smuggle him"—then it also helps to unravel some of the difficulties in the question of Pierre's motivation. Ostensibly he joins the insurrectionists because Antonio has bedded with Aquilina, and the Senate has rebuked him for assaulting Antonio. This would make Pierre an emotional and vindictive figure. But nowhere does he behave to Aquilina as if she were particularly dear to him, and his speeches usually have about them an air of heroic idealism (thinly overlaid with cynicism). But it is Jaffeir, not Pierre, who introduces Aquilina as the motive for Pierre's rebellion, thus merely providing the other man with the same motivation that he himself feels. Nowhere, except when playing on Jaffeir's sensibilities, does Pierre seem to behave as if she were the prime cause of his discontent. He is angered at the way the Senate has treated him, but Quin was right to play him as a gallant man and an idealist, it being part of the code of a gentleman never to admit his idealism. There is often a division between what

---

[21] See R. E. Hughes, " 'Comic Relief' in Otway's 'Venice Preserv'd'," *Notes and Queries*, CCIII (1958), 65–66; and especially William H. McBurney (note 8, above).

Otway's characters say and what they do, what they are and what they appear to be.

This is not necessarily a dramatic fault. If an actor is to make sense of the entirety of a part, he is likely to ask not only how he should say his lines, but why he should say them. If he does not he will probably rant. Nothing in the stage history of *Venice Preserved* suggests that the performances of a Garrick or a Siddons were bombastic. On the contrary, within the conventions of the stage at their time, they were found natural and moving. Theatrical action can suggest latent motives and realize concealed forces not easily apparent in the study. (Garrick's Jaffeir, begging in splendid dress, clearly epitomizes the power of the actor to fuse disparate elements together.) Although the dramatic conventions of the heroic stage cannot now be recreated, if a way to the unfamiliar through the familiar can be found, then the closest parallel to Otway may not be in Jacobean tragedy at all, but in the drama of Ibsen, and above all of Strindberg.[22]

MALCOLM KELSALL

University of Reading

[22] Not enough is known of Otway's affair with Elizabeth Barry to justify a psychological criticism of the origins of the play, but a parallel with Strindberg's tangled emotional life is not without justification.

VENICE PRESERVED

Epistle Dedicatory
To Her Grace the Duchess of Portsmouth

MADAM,

Were it possible for me to let the world know how entirely
your Grace's goodness has devoted a poor man to your
service, were there words enough in speech to express the
mighty sense I have of your great bounty towards me,   5
surely I should write and talk of it forever; but your Grace
has given me so large a theme, and laid so very vast a
foundation, that imagination wants stock to build upon it.
I am as one dumb when I would speak of it, and when I
strive to write, I want a scale of thought sufficient to com-   10
prehend the height of it. Forgive me then, madam, if (as a
poor peasant once made a present of an apple to an emperor) I bring this small tribute, the humble growth of my
little garden, and lay it at your feet. Believe it is paid you
with the utmost gratitude, believe that so long as I have   15
thought to remember how very much I owe your generous
nature, I will ever have a heart that shall be grateful for it
too. Your Grace, next Heaven, deserves it amply from me;
that gave me life, but on a hard condition, till your extended favor taught me to prize the gift, and took the heavy   20
burden it was clogged with from me: I mean hard fortune.
When I had enemies that with malicious power kept back
and shaded me from those royal beams, whose warmth is all
I have, or hope to live by, your noble pity and compassion
found me where I was far cast backward from my blessing,   25
down in the rear of fortune; called me up, placed me in the
shine, and I have felt its comfort. You have in that restored
me to my native right, for a steady faith, and loyalty to my
prince, was all the inheritance my father left me, and however hardly my ill-fortune deal with me, 'tis what I prize so   30
well that I ne'er pawned it yet, and hope I ne'er shall part

Duchess of Portsmouth] Louise Renée de Kéroualle (1649–1734), Charles
II's French mistress.
12–13. *apple to an emperor*] given to Theodosius II, emperor of the Eastern
Roman Empire. He gave it to the empress, she presented it to her supposed
lover Paulinus, and he then offered it to the emperor, who had him exe-
cuted. (An instance of Otway's lack of tact?)

with it. Nature and Fortune were certainly in league when you were born, and as the first took care to give you beauty enough to enslave the hearts of all the world, so the other resolved to do its merit justice, that none but a monarch, fit 35 to rule that world, should e'er possess it, and in it he had an empire. The young prince you have given him, by his blooming virtues, early declares the mighty stock he came from; and as you have taken all the pious care of a dear mother and a prudent guardian to give him a noble and 40 generous education, may it succeed according to his merits and your wishes. May he grow up to be a bulwark to his illustrious father, and a patron to his loyal subjects, with wisdom and learning to assist him, whenever called to his councils, to defend his right against the encroachments of 45 republicans in his senates, to cherish such men as shall be able to vindicate the royal cause, that good and fit servants to the Crown may never be lost for want of a protector. May he have courage and conduct, fit to fight his battles abroad and terrify his rebels at home; and that all these may 50 be yet more sure, may he never, during the springtime of his years, when those growing virtues ought with care to be cherished in order to their ripening; may he never meet with vicious natures, or the tongues of faithless, sordid, insipid flatterers to blast 'em. To conclude: may he be as 55 great as the hand of fortune (with his honor) shall be able to make him; and may your Grace, who are so good a mistress, and so noble a patroness, never meet with a less grateful servant, than,

Madam,   60
Your Grace's entirely
Devoted Creature,
THOMAS OTWAY

PROLOGUE

In these distracted times, when each man dreads
The bloody stratagems of busy heads;
When we have feared three years we know not what,⎫
Till witnesses begin to die o'th' rot,   ⎬
What made our poet meddle with a plot?   ⎭   5
Was't that he fancied, for the very sake
And name of plot, his trifling play might take?
For there's not in't one inch-board evidence,⎫
But 'tis, he says, to reason plain and sense,   ⎬
And that he thinks a plausible defense.   ⎭   10
Were truth by sense and reason to be tried,
Sure all our swearers might be laid aside.
No, of such tools our author has no need,
To make his plot, or make his play succeed;
He of black bills has no prodigious tales,   15
Or Spanish pilgrims cast ashore in Wales;
Here's not one murdered magistrate at least,
Kept rank like ven'son for a City feast,
Grown four days stiff, the better to prepare
And fit his pliant limbs to ride in chair.   20

1. distracted] *Q1–3, W*; unsettled *F1–2*.
3. we know] *F1, Q1–3, W*; I know *F2*.
4. begin] *F2, Q1–3, W*; began *F1*.
5. made] *F2, Q1–3, W*; makes *F1*.
9. 'tis, he says, to] *F1, Q1–3, W*; is to each man's *F2*.
10. plausible] *F2, Q1–3, W*; plentiful *F1*.

14. or make] *F1–2, Q3, W*; or may *Q1–2*.
16. cast] *Q1–3, W*; thrown *F1–2*.
20.] *After l. 20, F1–2 read:* He has [Here are *F2*] no truths of such a monstrous stature, / And some believe there are none such in Nature.

---

3. *three years*] Titus Oates made his first revelations of the Popish Plot to the Privy Council in September, 1678.

8. *inch-board evidence*] evidence sworn to with great force, i.e., able to penetrate a board an inch thick.

15. *black bills*] a sort of halberd or axe-headed pike.

16. *Spanish pilgrims*] William Bedloe, the informer, claimed that the Jesuits planned to land an army of Irish soldiers disguised as Spanish pilgrims in Wales (see Roger L'Estrange, *The History of the Plot* [London, 1679], p. 51).

17. *murdered magistrate*] Sir Edmund Berry Godfrey. Lines 19–20 allude to the story that his body was removed from Somerset House in a sedan chair three days after his murder (*The History of the Plot*, p. 65).

Yet here's an army raised, though under ground,
But no man seen, nor one commission found;
Here is a traitor too, that's very old,
Turbulent, subtle, mischievous and bold,
Bloody, revengeful, and to crown his part,   25
Loves fumbling with a wench with all his heart;
Till after having many changes passed,
In spite of age (thanks Heaven) is hanged at last.
Next is a Senator that keeps a whore,
In Venice none a higher office bore;   30
To lewdness every night the lecher ran,⎫
Show me, all London, such another man,⎬
Match him at Mother Creswold's if you can.⎭
Oh Poland, Poland! had it been thy lot,
T' have heard in time of this Venetian plot,   35
Thou surely chosen hadst one king from thence,
And honored them as thou hast England since.

21. Yet] *Q1–3, W*; But *F1–2*.
22. But] *Q1–3, W*; Yet *F1–2*.
22. man] *F1, Q1–3, W*; men *F2*.
27. Till] *Q1–3, W*; And *F1–2*.
28. In spite . . . is] *Q1–2*; Thanks Heav'n, for all his age, he's *F1*; In spite of age (thanks Heav'n) he's *F2*; In spite of age (thanks t'Heav'n) is *Q3, W*.
29. Next is] *Q1–3, W*; Next, there's *F1*; Next, here's *F2*.
30. higher] *F2, Q1–3, W*; greater *F1*.
32. all] *F1, Q1–3, W*; in *F2*.
34. Oh] *F1, Q1–3, W*; Ah *F2*.

22. *commission*] The Pope was supposed to have sent to England commissions for raising a rebellious army (see Titus Oates, *A True Narrative of the Horrid Plot* [London, 1679], p. 61).
33. *Creswold*] or Creswell, a notorious procuress.
34. *Poland*] Tory satire alleged that Shaftesbury had aspired to the Polish throne at the election of 1675.

PERSONAE DRAMATIS

DUKE OF VENICE	*Mr. D. Williams*
PRIULI, father to Belvidera, a Senator	*Mr. Boman*
ANTONIO, a fine speaker in the Senate	*Mr. Leigh*
JAFFEIR	*Mr. Betterton*
PIERRE	*Mr. Smith*
RENAULT	*Mr. Wilshire*
BEDAMORE	*Mr. Gillo*
SPINOSA	*Mr. Percival*

THEODORE
ELIOT
REVELLIDO
DURAND   } Conspirators
MEZZANA
BRAINVEIL
TERNON
BRABE
[RETROSI]

BELVIDERA	*Mrs. Barry*
AQUILINA	*Mrs. Currer*

TWO WOMEN, Attendants on Belvidera
TWO WOMEN, Servants to Aquilina
THE COUNCIL OF TEN
OFFICER
GUARDS
FRIAR
EXECUTIONER AND RABBLE

Venice Preserved

or

A Plot Discovered

ACT I

[I]   *Enter* Priuli *and* Jaffeir.

PRIULI.

   No more! I'll hear no more. Begone and leave.

JAFFEIR.

   Not hear me! By my sufferings but you shall!
   My lord, my lord; I'm not that abject wretch
   You think me. Patience! Where's the distance throws
   Me back so far, but I may boldly speak   5
   In right, though proud oppression will not hear me!

PRIULI.

   Have you not wronged me?

JAFFEIR.   Could my nature e'er
   Have brooked injustice or the doing wrongs,
   I need not now thus low have bent myself
   To gain a hearing from a cruel father!   10
   Wronged you?

PRIULI.   Yes! wronged me, in the nicest point:
   The honor of my house; you have done me wrong.
   You may remember (for I now will speak,
   And urge its baseness), when you first came home
   From travel, with such hopes as made you looked on   15
   By all men's eyes, a youth of expectation;
   Pleased with your growing virtue, I received you,
   Courted, and sought to raise you to your merits.
   My house, my table, nay my fortune too,
   My very self, was yours; you might have used me   20
   To your best service. Like an open friend,

I treated, trusted you, and thought you mine;
When in requital of my best endeavors,
You treacherously practiced to undo me,
Seduced the weakness of my age's darling,   25
My only child, and stole her from my bosom.
Oh Belvidera!
JAFFEIR.   'Tis to me you owe her,
Childless you had been else, and in the grave
Your name extinct, nor no more Priuli heard of.
You may remember, scarce five years are past,   30
Since in your brigantine you sailed to see
The Adriatic wedded by our Duke,
And I was with you. Your unskilful pilot
Dashed us upon a rock; when to your boat
You made for safety, entered first yourself;   35
The affrighted Belvidera following next,
As she stood trembling on the vessel side,
Was by a wave washed off into the deep—
When instantly I plunged into the sea,
And buffeting the billows to her rescue,   40
Redeemed her life with half the loss of mine.
Like a rich conquest in one hand I bore her,
And with the other dashed the saucy waves
That thronged and pressed to rob me of my prize.
I brought her, gave her to your despairing arms;   45
Indeed you thanked me; but a nobler gratitude
Rose in her soul: for from that hour she loved me,
Till for her life she paid me with herself.
PRIULI.
You stole her from me, like a thief you stole her,
At dead of night; that cursed hour you chose   50
To rifle me of all my heart held dear.
May all your joys in her prove false like mine;
A sterile fortune, and a barren bed,
Attend you both; continual discord make
Your days and nights bitter and grievous; still   55

---

32. *Adriatic wedded*] the ceremony on Ascension Day in which the Doge
cast a ring into the sea to symbolize that Venetian power was "wedded" to
the ocean.

May the hard hand of a vexatious need
Oppress, and grind you; till at last you find
The curse of disobedience all your portion.

JAFFEIR.
Half of your curse you have bestowed in vain,
Heav'n has already crowned our faithful loves   60
With a young boy, sweet as his mother's beauty.
May he live to prove more gentle than his grandsire,
And happier than his father!

PRIULI.   Rather live
To bait thee for his bread, and din your ears
With hungry cries; whilst his unhappy mother   65
Sits down and weeps in bitterness of want.

JAFFEIR.
You talk as if it would please you.

PRIULI.   'Twould, by Heav'n.
Once she was dear indeed; the drops that fell
From my sad heart when she forgot her duty!
The fountain of my life was not so precious;   70
But she is gone, and if I am a man
I will forget her.

JAFFEIR.
Would I were in my grave.

PRIULI.   And she too with thee;
For, living here, you're but my cursed remembrancers
I once was happy.   75

JAFFEIR.
You use me thus, because you know my soul
Is fond of Belvidera. You perceive
My life feeds on her, therefore thus you treat me.
Oh! could my soul ever have known satiety!
Were I that thief, the doer of such wrongs   80
As you upbraid me with, what hinders me,
But I might send her back to you with contumely,
And court my fortune where she would be kinder!

PRIULI.
You dare not do't.—

JAFFEIR.   Indeed, my lord, I dare not.
My heart that awes me is too much my master.   85
Three years are past since first our vows were plighted,

During which time, the world must bear me witness,
I have treated Belvidera like your daughter,
The daughter of a Senator of Venice.
Distinction, place, attendance, and observance,   90
Due to her birth, she always has commanded.
Out of my little fortune I have done this,
Because (though hopeless e'er to win your nature)
The world might see I loved her for herself,
Not as the heiress of the great Priuli.—   95

PRIULI.
No more!

JAFFEIR.   Yes! all, and then adieu forever.
There's not a wretch that lives on common charity
But's happier than me: for I have known
The luscious sweets of plenty, every night
Have slept with soft content about my head,   100
And never waked but to a joyful morning;
Yet now must fall like a full ear of corn,
Whose blossom 'scaped, yet's withered in the ripening.

PRIULI.
Home and be humble, study to retrench;
Discharge the lazy vermin of thy hall,   105
Those pageants of thy folly;
Reduce the glittering trappings of thy wife
To humble weeds, fit for thy little state;
Then to some suburb cottage both retire;
Drudge, to feed loathsome life: get brats, and starve—   110
Home, home, I say.—   *Exit* Priuli.

JAFFEIR.   Yes, if my heart would let me,
This proud, this swelling heart, home I would go,
But that my doors are hateful to my eyes,
Filled and dammed up with gaping creditors,
Watchful as fowlers when their game will spring.   115
I have now not fifty ducats in the world,
Yet still I am in love, and pleased with ruin.
Oh Belvidera! Oh she's my wife—
And we will bear our wayward fate together,
But ne'er know comfort more.

Enter Pierre.

2+   –11–

PIERRE.   My friend, good morrow!   120
    How fares the honest partner of my heart?
    What, melancholy! Not a word to spare me?

JAFFEIR.
    I'm thinking, Pierre, how that damned starving quality
    Called honesty, got footing in the world.

PIERRE.
    Why, pow'rful villainy first set it up,   125
    For its own ease and safety; honest men
    Are the soft easy cushions on which knaves
    Repose and fatten. Were all mankind villains,
    They'd starve each other; lawyers would want practice,
    Cut-throats rewards; each man would kill his brother   130
    Himself, none would be paid or hanged for murder.
    Honesty was a cheat invented first
    To bind the hands of bold deserving rogues,
    That fools and cowards might sit safe in power,
    And lord it uncontrolled above their betters.   135

JAFFEIR.
    Then honesty is but a notion.

PIERRE.   Nothing else.
    Like wit, much talked of, not to be defined;
    He that pretends to most too, has least share in't;
    'Tis a ragged virtue. Honesty! No more on't.

JAFFEIR.
    Sure thou art honest?

PIERRE.   So indeed men think me,   140
    But they're mistaken, Jaffeir: I am a rogue
    As well as they;
    A fine gay bold-faced villain, as thou seest me.
    'Tis true, I pay my debts when they're contracted;
    I steal from no man; would not cut a throat   145
    To gain admission to a great man's purse,
    Or a whore's bed; I'd not betray my friend
    To get his place or fortune; I scorn to flatter
    A blown-up fool above me, or crush the wretch beneath me,
    Yet, Jaffeir, for all this, I am a villain!   150

JAFFEIR.
    A villain—

PIERRE.   Yes, a most notorious villain:

To see the suff'rings of my fellow creatures,
And own myself a man; to see our Senators
Cheat the deluded people with a show
Of liberty, which yet they ne'er must taste of.   155
They say, by them our hands are free from fetters,
Yet whom they please they lay in basest bonds;
Bring whom they please to infamy and sorrow;
Drive us like wracks down the rough tide of power,
Whilst no hold's left to save us from destruction.   160
All that bear this are villains; and I one,
Not to rouse up at the great call of nature,
And check the growth of these domestic spoilers,
That make us slaves and tell us 'tis our charter.

AFFEIR.

Oh Aquilina! Friend, to lose such beauty,   165
The dearest purchase of thy noble labors;
She was thy right by conquest, as by love.

PIERRE.

Oh Jaffeir! I'd so fixed my heart upon her,
That wheresoe'er I framed a scheme of life
For time to come, she was my only joy   170
With which I wished to sweeten future cares.
I fancied pleasures, none but one that loves
And dotes as I did can imagine like 'em—
When in the extremity of all these hopes,
In the most charming hour of expectation,   175
Then when our eager wishes soar the highest,
Ready to stoop and grasp the lovely game,
A haggard owl, a worthless kite of prey,
With his foul wings sailed in and spoiled my quarry.

JAFFEIR.

I know the wretch, and scorn him as thou hat'st him.   180

PIERRE

Curse on the common good that's so protected,
Where every slave that heaps up wealth enough
To do much wrong, becomes a lord of right!
I, who believed no ill could e'er come near me,

164. make . . . tell] Q3, W; makes
. . . tells Q1–2.

Found in the embraces of my Aquilina   185
A wretched old but itching Senator,
A wealthy fool, that had bought out my title,
A rogue, that uses beauty like a lambskin,
Barely to keep him warm; that filthy cuckoo too
Was in my absence crept into my nest,   190
And spoiling all my brood of noble pleasure.

JAFFEIR.

Didst thou not chase him thence?

PIERRE.   I did, and drove
The rank old bearded hirco stinking home.
The matter was complained of in the Senate,
I summoned to appear, and censured basely,   195
For violating something they call *privilege*—
This was the recompense of my service!
Would I'd been rather beaten by a coward!
A soldier's mistress, Jaffeir, 's his religion,
When that's profaned, all other ties are broken,   200
That even dissolves all former bonds of service,
And from that hour I think myself as free
To be the foe as ere the friend of Venice—
Nay, dear revenge, when e'er thou call'st I am ready.

JAFFEIR.

I think no safety can be here for virtue,   205
And grieve my friend as much as thou to live
In such a wretched state as this of Venice,
When all agree to spoil the public good,
And villains fatten with the brave man's labors.

PIERRE.

We have neither safety, unity, nor peace,   210
For the foundation's lost of common good;
Justice is lame as well as blind amongst us;
The laws (corrupted to their ends that make 'em)
Serve but for instruments of some new tyranny
That every day starts up to enslave us deeper.   215
Now could this glorious cause but find out friends
To do it right! Oh Jaffeir! then might'st thou
Not wear these seals of woe upon thy face;

---

193. *hirco*] a he-goat.

The proud Priuli should be taught humanity,
And learn to value such a son as thou art.   220
I dare not speak! But my heart bleeds this moment!

JAFFEIR.

Cursed be the cause, though I thy friend be part on't!
Let me partake the troubles of thy bosom,
For I am used to misery, and perhaps
May find a way to sweeten't to thy spirit.   225

PIERRE.

Too soon it will reach thy knowledge—

JAFFEIR.   Then from thee
Let it proceed. There's virtue in thy friendship
Would make the saddest tale of sorrow pleasing,
Strengthen my constancy, and welcome ruin.

PIERRE.

Then thou art ruined!

JAFFEIR.   That I long since knew;   230
I and ill fortune have been long acquaintance.

PIERRE.

I passed this very moment by thy doors,
And found them guarded by a troop of villains;
The sons of public rapine were destroying.
They told me, by the sentence of the law   235
They had commission to seize all thy fortune,
Nay more, Priuli's cruel hand hath signed it.
Here stood a ruffian with a horrid face
Lording it o'er a pile of massy plate,
Tumbled into a heap for public sale;   240
There was another making villainous jests
At thy undoing; he had ta'en possession
Of all thy ancient most domestic ornaments,
Rich hangings, intermixed and wrought with gold;
The very bed, which on thy wedding night   245
Received thee to the arms of Belvidera,
The scene of all thy joys, was violated
By the coarse hands of filthy dungeon villains,
And thrown amongst the common lumber.

JAFFEIR.

Now thanks Heav'n—   250

PIERRE.

    Thank Heav'n! For what?

JAFFEIR.   That I am not worth a ducat.

PIERRE.

    Curse thy dull stars, and the worse fate of Venice,
    Where brothers, friends, and fathers, all are false;
    Where there's no trust, no truth; where innocence
    Stoops under vile oppression, and vice lords it.   255
    Hadst thou but seen, as I did, how at last
    Thy beauteous Belvidera, like a wretch
    That's doomed to banishment, came weeping forth,
    Shining through tears, like April suns in showers
    That labor to o'ercome the cloud that loads 'em,   260
    Whilst two young virgins, on whose arms she leaned,
    Kindly looked up, and at her grief grew sad,
    As if they catched the sorrows that fell from her.
    Even the lewd rabble that were gathered round
    To see the sight, stood mute when they beheld her,   265
    Governed their roaring throats and grumbled pity.
    I could have hugged the greasy rogues; they pleased me.

JAFFEIR.

    I thank thee for this story from my soul,
    Since now I know the worst that can befall me.
    Ah Pierre! I have a heart that could have borne   270
    The roughest wrong my fortune could have done me;
    But when I think what Belvidera feels,
    The bitterness her tender spirit tastes of,
    I own myself a coward. Bear my weakness,
    If throwing thus my arms about thy neck,   275
    I play the boy, and blubber in thy bosom.
    Oh! I shall drown thee with my sorrows!

PIERRE.   Burn!

    First burn, and level Venice to thy ruin!
    What, starve like beggars' brats in frosty weather,
    Under a hedge, and whine ourselves to death!   280
    Thou, or thy cause, shall never want assistance,
    Whilst I have blood or fortune fit to serve thee.
    Command my heart: thou art every way its master.

JAFFEIR.

    No. There's a secret pride in bravely dying.

PIERRE.

   Rats die in holes and corners, dogs run mad;   285
   Man knows a braver remedy for sorrow:
   Revenge! the attribute of gods; they stamped it
   With their great image on our natures. Die!
   Consider well the cause that calls upon thee;
   And if thou art base enough, die then. Remember   290
   Thy Belvidera suffers. Belvidera!
   Die—damn first—What, be decently interred
   In a churchyard, and mingle thy brave dust
   With stinking rogues that rot in dirty winding sheets,
   Surfeit-slain fools, the common dung o'th' soil!   295

JAFFEIR.

   Oh!

PIERRE. Well said, out with't, swear a little—

JAFFEIR.   Swear!
   By sea and air! by earth, by Heaven and Hell,
   I will revenge my Belvidera's tears!
   Hark thee, my friend—Priuli—is—a Senator!

PIERRE.

   A dog!

JAFFEIR.   Agreed.

PIERRE.   Shoot him.

JAFFEIR.   With all my heart.   300
   No more. Where shall we meet at night?

PIERRE.   I'll tell thee:
   On the Rialto every night at twelve
   I take my evening's walk of meditation,
   There we two will meet, and talk of precious
   Mischief—   305

JAFFEIR.

   Farewell.

PIERRE.   At twelve.

JAFFEIR.   At any hour. My plagues
   Will keep me waking.   *Exit* Pierre.
                   Tell me why, good Heav'n,
   Thou mad'st me what I am, with all the spirit,
   Aspiring thoughts and elegant desires
   That fill the happiest man? Ah! rather why   310
   Didst thou not form me sordid as my fate,

Base-minded, dull, and fit to carry burdens?
Why have I sense to know the curse that's on me?
Is this just dealing, Nature? Belvidera!

Enter Belvidera [*with two Attendants*].

Poor Belvidera!

BELVIDERA.   Lead me, lead me, my virgins,   315
To that kind voice! My lord, my love, my refuge!
Happy my eyes, when they behold thy face;
My heavy heart will leave its doleful beating
At sight of thee, and bound with sprightful joys.
Oh smile, as when our loves were in their spring,   320
And cheer my fainting soul.

JAFFEIR.   As when our loves
Were in their spring? Has then my fortune changed?
Art thou not Belvidera, still the same,
Kind, good, and tender, as my arms first found thee?
If thou art altered, where shall I have harbor?   325
Where ease my loaded heart? Oh! where complain?

BELVIDERA.

Does this appear like change, or love decaying?
When thus I throw myself into thy bosom,
With all the resolution of a strong truth,
Beats not my heart, as 'twould alarm thine   330
To a new charge of bliss? I joy more in thee
Than did thy mother when she hugged thee first,
And blessed the gods for all her travail past.

JAFFEIR.

Can there in Woman be such glorious faith?
Sure all ill stories of thy sex are false.   335
Oh Woman! lovely Woman! Nature made thee
To temper Man: we had been brutes without you.
Angels are painted fair, to look like you;
There's in you all that we believe of Heav'n,
Amazing brightness, purity and truth,   340
Eternal joy, and everlasting love.

BELVIDERA.

If love be treasure, we'll be wond'rous rich,
I have so much, my heart will surely break with't;
Vows cannot express it, when I would declare

How great's my joy, I am dumb with the big thought;   345
I swell, and sigh, and labor with my longing.
Oh lead me to some desert wide and wild,
Barren as our misfortunes, where my soul
May have its vent; where I may tell aloud
To the high heavens, and every list'ning planet,   350
With what a boundless stock my bosom's fraught;
Where I may throw my eager arms about thee,
Give loose to love with kisses, kindling joy,
And let off all the fire that's in my heart.

JAFFEIR.

Oh Belvidera! double I am a beggar,   355
Undone by fortune, and in debt to thee.
Want! worldly want! that hungry meagre fiend
Is at my heels, and chases me in view.
Canst thou bear cold and hunger? Can these limbs,
Framed for the tender offices of love,   360
Endure the bitter gripes of smarting poverty?
When banished by our miseries abroad
(As suddenly we shall be) to seek out
(In some far climate where our names are strangers)
For charitable succor; wilt thou then,   365
When in a bed of straw we shrink together,
And the bleak winds shall whistle round our heads;
Wilt thou then talk thus to me? Wilt thou then
Hush my cares thus, and shelter me with love?

BELVIDERA.

Oh I will love thee, even in madness love thee;   370
Though my distracted senses should forsake me,
I'd find some intervals when my poor heart
Should 'suage itself and be let loose to thine.
Though the bare earth be all our resting-place,
Its roots our food, some clift our habitation,   375
I'll make this arm a pillow for thy head;
As thou sighing ly'st, and swelled with sorrow,
Creep to thy bosom, pour the balm of love
Into thy soul, and kiss thee to thy rest;
Then praise our God, and watch thee till the morning.   380

JAFFEIR.

Hear this, you Heavens, and wonder how you made her!

Reign, reign, ye monarchs that divide the world.
Busy rebellion ne'er will let you know
Tranquillity and happiness like mine.
Like gaudy ships, th'obsequious billows fall 385
And rise again, to lift you in your pride;
They wait but for a storm and then devour you.
I, in my private bark, already wrecked,
Like a poor merchant driven on unknown land,
That had by chance packed up his choicest treasure 390
In one dear casket, and saved only that:
Since I must wander further on the shore,
Thus hug my little, but my precious store,
Resolved to scorn, and trust my fate no more.   *Exeunt.*

ACT II

Enter Pierre *and* Aquilina.

AQUILINA.
   By all thy wrongs, thou art dearer to my arms
   Than all the wealth of Venice. Prithee stay,
   And let us love tonight.
PIERRE.   No. There's fool,
   There's fool about thee. When a woman sells
   Her flesh to fools, her beauty's lost to me;   5
   They leave a taint, a sully where they've passed.
   There's such a baneful quality about 'em,
   Even spoils complexions with their own nauseousness;
   They infect all they touch. I cannot think
   Of tasting anything a fool has palled.   10
AQUILINA.
   I loath and scorn that fool thou mean'st, as much
   Or more than thou canst, but the beast has gold
   That makes him necessary; power too,
   To qualify my character, and poise me
   Equal with peevish virtue that beholds   15
   My liberty with envy. In their hearts
   They're loose as I am; but an ugly power
   Sits in their faces, and frights pleasures from 'em.
PIERRE.
   Much good may't do you, madam, with your Senator.
AQUILINA.
   My Senator! Why, canst thou think that wretch   20
   E'er filled thy Aquilina's arms with pleasure?
   Think'st thou, because I sometimes give him leave
   To foil himself at what he is unfit for,
   Because I force myself to endure and suffer him,
   Think'st thou I love him? No, by all the joys   25
   Thou ever gav'st me, his presence is my penance;
   The worst thing an old man can be's a lover,
   A mere *memento mori* to poor woman.
   I never lay by his decrepit side,

17. They're] *Q3, W*; Are *Q1–2*.

But all that night I pondered on my grave.   30
PIERRE.
    Would he were well sent thither.
AQUILINA.   That's my wish too:
    For then, my Pierre, I might have cause with pleasure
    To play the hypocrite. Oh! how I could weep
    Over the dying dotard, and kiss him too,
    In hopes to smother him quite. Then, when the time   35
    Was come to pay my sorrows at his funeral
    (For he has already made me heir to treasures
    Would make me out-act a real widow's whining),
    How could I frame my face to fit my mourning!
    With wringing hands attend him to his grave,   40
    Fall swooning on his hearse; take mad possession
    Even of the dismal vault where he lay buried;
    There like the Ephesian matron dwell, till thou,
    My lovely soldier, comest to my deliverance;
    Then throwing up my veil, with open arms   45
    And laughing eyes, run to new dawning joy.
PIERRE.
    No more! I have friends to meet me here tonight,
    And must be private. As you prize my friendship,
    Keep up your coxcomb. Let him not pry nor listen,
    Nor fisk about the house as I have seen him,   50
    Like a tame mumping squirrel, with a bell on;
    Curs will be abroad to bite him if you do.
AQUILINA.
    What friends to meet? May I not be of your council?
PIERRE.
    How! a woman ask questions out of bed?
    Go to your Senator, ask him what passes   55
    Amongst his brethren, he'll hide nothing from you;
    But pump not me for politics. No more!
    Give order that whoever in my name
    Comes here, receive admittance. So, goodnight.

---

    43. *Ephesian matron*] She lamented her husband in his tomb, but was
seduced there by a soldier. See Petronius, *Satyricon*, cap. cxi–cxii.
    50. *fisk*] jump.
    51. *mumping*] mumbling; nibbling.

AQUILINA.

Must we ne'er meet again! Embrace no more!   60
Is love so soon and utterly forgotten!

PIERRE.

As you henceforward treat your fool I'll think on't.

AQUILINA.

Cursed be all fools, and doubly cursed myself,
The worst of fools. —I die if he forsakes me;
And now to keep him, Heaven or Hell instruct me.   *Exeunt.*   65

[II.ii]   *Scene, The Rialto.*
                Enter Jaffeir.

JAFFEIR.

I am here, and thus, the shades of night around me,
I look as if all Hell were in my heart,
And I in Hell. Nay, surely 'tis so with me:
For every step I tread, methinks some fiend
Knocks at my breast, and bids it not be quiet.   5
I've heard how desperate wretches, like myself,
Have wandered out at this dead time of night
To meet the foe of mankind in his walk.
Sure I am so cursed that, though of heav'n forsaken,
No minister of darkness cares to tempt me.   10
Hell! Hell! why sleepest thou?

                Enter Pierre.

PIERRE.

Sure I have stayed too long:
The clock has struck, and I may lose my proselyte.
Speak, who goes there?

JAFFEIR.   A dog, that comes to howl
At yonder moon. What's he that asks the question?   15

PIERRE.

A friend to dogs, for they are honest creatures,
And ne'er betray their masters; never fawn
On any that they love not. Well met, friend.
Jaffeir!

JAFFEIR.   The same. Oh Pierre! Thou art come in season,
I was just going to pray.

PIERRE.   Ah that's mechanic,   20
    Priests make a trade on't, and yet starve by it too.
    No praying, it spoils business, and time's precious.
    Where's Belvidera?
JAFFEIR.   For a day or two
    I've lodged her privately, till I see farther
    What fortune will do with me. Prithee, friend,   25
    If thou wouldst have me fit to hear good counsel,
    Speak not of Belvidera—
PIERRE.   Speak not of her?
JAFFEIR.
    Oh no!
PIERRE.   Nor name her? Maybe I wish her well.
JAFFEIR.
    Who well?
PIERRE.   Thy wife, thy lovely Belvidera.
    I hope a man may wish his friend's wife well,   30
    And no harm done!
JAFFEIR.   Y'are merry, Pierre!
PIERRE.   I am so.
    Thou shalt smile too, and Belvidera smile;
    We'll all rejoice. Here's something to buy pins;
    Marriage is chargeable.
JAFFEIR.   I but half wished
    To see the Devil, and he's here already.   35
    Well!
    What must this buy, rebellion, murder, treason?
    Tell me which way I must be damned for this.
PIERRE.
    When last we parted we had no qualms like these,
    But entertained each other's thoughts like men   40
    Whose souls were well acquainted. Is the world
    Reformed since our last meeting? What new miracles
    Have happened? Has Priuli's heart relented?
    Can he be honest?
JAFFEIR.   Kind Heav'n! let heavy curses

33.] *Q3, W adds* S.D. *Gives him a
purse.*

34. *chargeable*] expensive.

Gall his old age; cramps, aches, rack his bones,   45
And bitterest disquiet wring his heart;
Oh let him live till life become his burden!
Let him groan under't long, linger an age
In the worst agonies and pangs of death,
And find its ease, but late.
PIERRE.   Nay, couldst thou not   50
As well, my friend, have stretched the curse to all
The Senate round, as to one single villain?
JAFFEIR.
But curses stick not. Could I kill with cursing,
By Heav'n I know not thirty heads in Venice
Should not be blasted; Senators should rot   55
Like dogs on dunghills; but their wives and daughters
Die of their own diseases. Oh for a curse
To kill with!
PIERRE.   Daggers, daggers, are much better!
JAFFEIR.
Ha!
PIERRE. Daggers.
JAFFEIR.   But where are they?
PIERRE.   Oh, a thousand
May be disposed in honest hands in Venice.   60
JAFFEIR.
Thou talk'st in clouds.
PIERRE.   But yet a heart half wronged,
As thine has been, would find the meaning, Jaffeir.
JAFFEIR.
A thousand daggers, all in honest hands;
And have not I a friend will stick one here?
PIERRE.
Yes, if I thought thou wert not to be cherished   65
To a nobler purpose, I'd be that friend.
But thou hast better friends, friends whom thy wrongs
Have made thy friends; friends, worthy to be called so.
I'll trust thee with a secret: there are spirits
This hour at work. But as thou art a man,   70
Whom I have picked and chosen from the world,
Swear that thou wilt be true to what I utter,
And when I have told thee that which only gods

-25-

And men like gods are privy to, then swear
No chance or change shall wrest it from thy bosom.   75

JAFFEIR.

When thou wouldst bind me, is there need of oaths?
(Green-sickness girls lose maidenheads with such counters)
For thou art so near my heart that thou mayst see
Its bottom, sounds its strength, and firmness to thee:
Is coward, fool, or villain, in my face?   80
If I seem none of these, I dare believe
Thou wouldst not use me in a little cause,
For I am fit for honor's toughest task,
Nor ever yet found fooling was my province;
And for a villainous inglorious enterprise,   85
I know thy heart so well, I dare lay mine
Before thee, set it to what point thou wilt.

PIERRE.

Nay, it's a cause thou wilt be fond of, Jaffeir.
For it is founded on the noblest basis,
Our liberties, our natural inheritance.   90
There's no religion, no hypocrisy in't;
We'll do the business, and ne'er fast and pray for't;
Openly act a deed the world shall gaze
With wonder at, and envy when it is done.

JAFFEIR.

For liberty!

PIERRE.   For liberty, my friend!   95
Thou shalt be freed from base Priuli's tyranny,
And thy sequestered fortunes healed again.
I shall be freed from opprobrious wrongs,
That press me now, and bend my spirit downward;
All Venice free, and every growing merit   100
Succeed to its just right. Fools shall be pulled
From Wisdom's seat: those baleful unclean birds,
Those lazy owls, who (perched near Fortune's top)
Sit only watchful with their heavy wings
To cuff down new-fledged virtues that would rise   105
To nobler heights, and make the grove harmonious.

JAFFEIR.

What can I do?

80. Is   coward]   *Q1–3*,   *W*;   A
coward *G*.

PIERRE.   Canst thou not kill a Senator?

JAFFEIR.
Were there one wise or honest, I could kill him
For herding with that nest of fools and knaves.
By all my wrongs, thou talk'st as if revenge   110
Were to be had, and the brave story warms me.

PIERRE.
Swear then!

JAFFEIR.   I do, by all those glittering stars,
And yond great ruling planet of the night!
By all good pow'rs above, and ill below!
By love and friendship, dearer than my life!   115
No pow'r or death shall make me false to thee.

PIERRE.
Here we embrace, and I'll unlock my heart.
A council's held hard by, where the destruction
Of this great empire's hatching. There I'll lead thee!
But be a man, for thou art to mix with men   120
Fit to disturb the peace of all the world,
And rule it when it's wildest.

JAFFEIR.   I give thee thanks
For this kind warning. Yes, I will be a man,
And charge thee, Pierre, when e'er thou see'st my fears
Betray me less, to rip this heart of mine   125
Out of my breast, and show it for a coward's.
Come, let's be gone, for from this hour I chase
All little thoughts, all tender human follies
Out of my bosom. Vengeance shall have room.
Revenge!

PIERRE.   And liberty!

JAFFEIR.   Revenge! Revenge—   *Exeunt.* 130

[II.iii]   *The scene changes to Aquilina's house, the Greek
                            courtesan.*

Enter Renault.

RENAULT.
Why was my choice ambition the first ground
A wretch can build on? It's indeed at distance

1. first] *Q1–2*; worst *Q3, W.*

A good prospect, tempting to the view;
The height delights us, and the mountain top
Looks beautiful because it's nigh to heav'n,   5
But we ne'er think how sandy's the foundation,
What storm will batter, and what tempest shake us!
Who's there?

Enter Spinosa.

SPINOSA.   Renault, good morrow! for by this time
     I think the scale of night has turned the balance,
     And weighs up morning. Has the clock struck twelve?   10
RENAULT.
     Yes, clocks will go as they are set; but Man,
     Irregular Man's ne'er constant, never certain.
     I've spent at least three precious hours of darkness
     In waiting dull attendance; 'tis the curse
     Of diligent virtue to be mixed like mine,   15
     With giddy tempers, souls but half resolved.
SPINOSA.
     Hell seize that soul amongst us it can frighten.
RENAULT.
     What's then the cause that I am here alone?
     Why are we not together?

Enter Eliot.

                         Oh sir, welcome!
     You are an Englishman; when treason's hatching   20
     One might have thought you'd not have been behind hand.
     In what whore's lap have you been lolling?
     Give but an Englishman his whore and ease,
     Beef and a sea-coal fire, he's yours forever.
ELIOT.
     Frenchman, you are saucy.
RENAULT.   How!

Enter Bedamore *the Ambassador,* Theodore, Brainveil, Durand, Brabe,
Revellido, Mezzana, Ternon, Retrosi, *Conspirators.*

BEDAMORE.   At difference, fie.   25
     Is this a time for quarrels? Thieves and rogues

---

24. *sea-coal*] coal brought by sea, as distinguished from charcoal.

Fall out and brawl. Should men of your high calling,
Men separated by the choice of providence
From the gross heap of mankind, and set here
In this great assembly as in one great jewel   30
T'adorn the bravest purpose it e'er smiled on;
Should you like boys wrangle for the trifles?

RENAULT.   Boys!

BEDAMORE.
    Renault, thy hand!

RENAULT.   I thought I'd given my heart
Long since to every man that mingles here,
But grieve to find it trusted with such tempers   35
That can't forgive my froward age its weakness.

BEDAMORE.
    Eliot, thou once hadst virtue. I have seen
Thy stubborn temper bend with godlike goodness
Not half thus courted: 'tis thy nation's glory
To hug the foe that offers brave alliance.   40
Once more embrace, my friends—we'll all embrace—
United thus, we are the mighty engine
Must twist this rooted empire from its basis!
Totters it not already?

ELIOT.   Would it were tumbling.

BEDAMORE.
    Nay, it shall down: this night we seal its ruin.   45

Enter Pierre.

Oh Pierre! thou art welcome!
Come to my breast, for by its hopes thou look'st
Lovelily dreadful, and the fate of Venice
Seems on thy sword already. Oh my Mars!
The poets that first feigned a God of War   50
Sure prophesied of thee.

PIERRE.   Friends! was not Brutus,
    (I mean that Brutus, who in open Senate

---

51. *Brutus*] Marcus Junius Brutus. Perhaps Otway wished to avoid any
suggestion that he meant Lucius Junius Brutus (the expeller of the Tar-
quins). Nathaniel Lee's play of that title had been suppressed in 1680 for its
revolutionary tendencies.

Stabbed the first Caesar that usurped the world)
A gallant man?

RENAULT.   Yes, and Catiline too,
Though story wrong his fame, for he conspired   55
To prop the reeling glory of his country;
His cause was good.

BEDAMORE.   And ours as much above it,
As Renault thou art superior to Cethegus,
Or Pierre to Cassius.

PIERRE.   Then to what we aim at.
When we do start? Or must we talk forever?   60

BEDAMORE.

No Pierre, the deed's near birth: fate seems to have set
The business up, and given it to our care.
I hope there's not a heart nor hand amongst us
But is firm and ready.

ALL.

    All! We'll die with Bedamore.

BEDAMORE.   Oh men,   65
Matchless, as will your glory be hereafter,
The game is for a matchless prize, if won;
If lost, disgraceful ruin.

RENAULT.   What can lose it?
The public stock's a beggar; one Venetian
Trusts not another. Look into their stores   70
Of general safety: empty magazines,
A tattered fleet, a murmuring unpaid army,
Bankrupt nobility, a harassed commonalty,
A factious, giddy, and divided Senate
Is all the strength of Venice: let's destroy it!   75
Let's fill their magazines with arms to awe them,
Man out their fleet, and make their trade maintain it;
Let loose the murmuring army on their masters,
To pay themselves with plunder; lop their nobles
To the base roots, whence most of 'em first sprung;   80
Enslave the rout, whom smarting will make humble;

---

54. *Catiline*] the notorious insurrectionist whose conspiracy was detected
by Cicero. Cethegus (l. 58) was also involved in the plot. His task was the
murder of the Senators.

Turn out their droning Senate, and possess
That seat of empire which our souls were framed for.

PIERRE.

Ten thousand men are armed at your nod,
Commanded all by leaders fit to guide   85
A battle for the freedom of the world;
This wretched state has starved them in its service,
And by your bounty quickened, they're resolved
To serve your glory, and revenge their own!
Th'have all their different quarters in this city,   90
Watch for th'alarm, and grumble 'tis so tardy.

BEDAMORE.

I doubt not, friend, but thy unwearied diligence
Has still kept waking and it shall have ease;
After this night it is resolved we meet
No more, till Venice own us for her lords.   95

PIERRE.

How lovely the Adriatic whore,
Dressed in her flames, will shine! Devouring flames!
Such as shall burn her to the watery bottom
And hiss in her foundation.

BEDAMORE.   Now if any
Amongst us that owns this glorious cause,   100
Have friends or interest he'd wish to save,
Let it be told. The general doom is sealed,
But I'd forgo the hopes of a world's empire,
Rather than wound the bowels of my friend.

PIERRE.

I must confess you there have touched my weakness.   105
I have a friend; hear it, such a friend!
My heart was ne'er shut to him. Nay, I'll tell you,
He knows the very business of this hour;
But he rejoices in the cause, and loves it.
W'have changed a vow to live and die together,   110
And he's at hand to ratify it here.

RENAULT.

How! All betrayed?

PIERRE.   No—I've dealt nobly with you;
I've brought my all into the public stock;
I had but one friend, and him I'll share amongst you!

Receive and cherish him. Or if, when seen   115
And searched, you find him worthless, as my tongue
Has lodged this secret in his faithful breast,
To ease your fears I wear a dagger here
Shall rip it out again, and give you rest.
Come forth, thou only good I e'er could boast of.   120

Enter Jaffeir *with a dagger.*

BEDAMORE.
His presence bears the show of manly virtue.
JAFFEIR.
I know you'll wonder all, that thus uncalled,
I dare approach this place of fatal counsels;
But I am amongst you, and by Heav'n it glads me
To see so many virtues thus united,   125
To restore justice and dethrone oppression.
Command this sword, if you would have it quiet,
Into this breast; but if you think it worthy
To cut the throats of reverend rogues in robes,
Send me into the cursed assembled Senate;   130
It shrinks not, though I meet a father there.
Would you behold this city flaming? Here's
A hand shall bear a lighted torch at noon
To the arsenal, and set its gates on fire.
RENAULT.
You talk this well, sir.
JAFFEIR.   Nay—by Heav'n, I'll do this!   135
Come, come, I read distrust in all your faces;
You fear me a villain, and indeed it's odd
To hear a stranger talk thus at first meeting
Of matters that have been so well debated;
But I come ripe with wrongs as you with counsels;   140
I hate this Senate, am a foe to Venice;
A friend to none but men resolved like me,
To push on mischief. Oh did you but know me,
I need not talk thus!
BEDAMORE.   Pierre! I must embrace him,
My heart beats to this man as if it knew him.   145
RENAULT.
I never loved these huggers.

JAFFEIR.   Still I see
  The cause delights me not. Your friends survey me
  As I were dang'rous—but I come armed
  Against all doubts, and to your trust will give
  A pledge, worth more than all the world can pay for.   150
  My Belvidera! Ho! my Belvidera!
BEDAMORE.
  What wonder next?
JAFFEIR.   Let me entreat you,
  As I have henceforth hopes to call ye friends,
  That all but the ambassador, this
  Grave guide of councils, with my friend that owns me,   155
  Withdraw a while to spare a woman's blushes.
                    Exeunt all but Bedamore, Renault, Jaffeir, Pierre.
BEDAMORE.
  Pierre, whither will this ceremony lead us?
JAFFEIR.
  My Belvidera! Belvidera!

                    Enter Belvidera.

BELVIDERA.
  Who calls so loud at this late peaceful hour?
  That voice was wont to come in gentler whispers,   160
  And fill my ears with the soft breath of love.
  Thou hourly image of my thoughts, where art thou?
JAFFEIR.
  Indeed 'tis late.
BELVIDERA.   Oh! I have slept, and dreamt,
  And dreamt again. Where hast thou been, thou loiterer?
  Though my eyes closed, my arms have still been opened,   165
  Stretched every way betwixt my broken slumbers,
  To search if thou wert come to crown my rest;
  There's no repose without thee. Oh the day
  Too soon will break, and wake us to our sorrow;
  Come, come to bed, and bid thy cares goodnight.   170
JAFFEIR.
  Oh Belvidera! we must change the scene

159. Who calls] *this edn.*; Who? /
Who calls *Q1–3, W.*

In which the past delights of life were tasted.
The poor sleep little. We must learn to watch
Our labors late, and early every morning,
Midst winter frosts, thin clad and fed with sparing,   175
Rise to our toils, and drudge away the day.

BELVIDERA.

Alas, where am I! Whither is't you lead me!
Methinks I read distraction in your face!
Something less gentle than the fate you tell me.
You shake and tremble too! Your blood runs cold!   180
Heavens guard my love, and bless his heart with patience.

JAFFEIR.

That I have patience, let our fate bear witness,
Who has ordained it so, that thou and I
(Thou the divinest good man e'er possessed,
And I the wretched'st of the race of man)   185
This very hour, without one tear, must part.

BELVIDERA.

Part! Must we part? Oh! am I then forsaken?
Will my love cast me off? Have my misfortunes
Offended him so highly that he'll leave me?
Why drag you from me? Whither are you going?   190
My dear! my life! my love!

JAFFEIR.   Oh friends!

BELVIDERA.   Speak to me.

JAFFEIR.

Take her from my heart,
She'll gain such hold else, I shall ne'er get loose.
I charge thee take her, but with tender'st care,
Relieve her troubles and assuage her sorrows.   195

RENAULT.

Rise, madam! and command amongst your servants!

JAFFEIR.

To you, sirs, and your honors, I bequeath her,
And with her this, when I prove unworthy—   *Gives a dagger.*
You know the rest—Then strike it to her heart,
And tell her, he, who three whole happy years   200
Lay in her arms, and each kind night repeated

175. thin clad] *W*; then clad *Q1–3*.

The passionate vows of still increasing love,
Sent that reward for all her truth and sufferings.

BELVIDERA.
Nay, take my life, since he has sold it cheaply;
Or send me to some distant clime your slave,   205
But let it be far off, lest my complainings
Should reach his guilty ears, and shake his peace.

JAFFEIR.
No, Belvidera, I've contrived thy honor.
Trust to my faith, and be but fortune kind
To me, as I'll preserve that faith unbroken,   210
When next we meet, I'll lift thee to a height
Shall gather all the gazing world about thee,
To wonder what strange virtue placed thee there.
But if we ne'er meet more—

BELVIDERA.   Oh thou unkind one,
Never meet more! Have I deserved this from you?   215
Look on me, tell me, tell me, speak, thou dear deceiver,
Why am I separated from thy love?
If I am false, accuse me; but if true,
Don't, prithee don't in poverty forsake me.
But pity the sad heart, that's torn with parting!   220
Yet hear me! yet recall me—

                    Exeunt Renault, Bedamore, *and* Belvidera.

JAFFEIR.   Oh my eyes!
Look not that way, but turn yourselves awhile
Into my heart, and be weaned all together.
My friend, where art thou?

PIERRE.   Here, my honor's brother.

JAFFEIR.
Is Belvidera gone?

PIERRE.   Renault has led her   225
Back to her own apartment; but, by Heav'n!
Thou must not see her more till our work's over.

JAFFEIR.
No!

PIERRE. Not for your life.

JAFFEIR.   Oh Pierre, wert thou but she,
How I could pull thee down into my heart,
Gaze on thee till my eye-strings cracked with love,   230

Till all my sinews with its fire extended,
Fixed me upon the rack of ardent longing;
Then swelling, sighing, raging to be blest,
Come like a panting turtle to thy breast,
On thy soft bosom, hovering, bill and play,   235
Confess the cause why last I fled away;
Own 'twas a fault, but swear to give it o'er,
And never follow false ambition more.   *Exeunt Ambo.*

ACT III

Enter Aquilina *and her* Maid.

AQUILINA.

　　Tell him I am gone to bed; tell him I am not at home; tell
　　him I've better company with me, or anything; tell him in
　　short I will not see him, the eternal troublesome vexatious
　　fool. He's worse company than an ignorant physician. I'll
　　not be disturbed at these unseasonable hours.　　　　　　5

MAID.

　　But madam! He's here already, just entered the doors.

AQUILINA.

　　Turn him out again, you unnecessary, useless, giddy-
　　brained ass! If he will not be gone, set the house afire and
　　burn us both. I had rather meet a toad in my dish than
　　that old hideous animal in my chamber tonight.　　　　10

　　　　　　　　　　　Enter Antonio.

ANTONIO.

　　Nacky, Nacky, Nacky—how dost do, Nacky? Hurry durry.
　　I am come, little Nacky; past eleven a clock, a late hour;
　　time in all conscience to go to bed, Nacky—Nacky did I say?
　　Ay Nacky; Aquilina, lina, lina, quilina, quilina, quilina,
　　Aquilina, Naquilina, Naquilina, Acky, Acky, Nacky,　　15
　　Nacky, Queen Nacky—come let's to bed—you fubbs, you
　　pug you—you little puss—purree tuzzey—I am a Senator.

AQUILINA.

　　You are a fool, I am sure.

ANTONIO.

　　May be so too, sweetheart. Never the worse Senator for all
　　that. Come Nacky, Nacky, let's have a game at rump,　　20
　　Nacky.

AQUILINA.

　　You would do well, Signor, to be troublesome here no
　　longer, but leave me to myself, be sober and go home, sir.

18. are a fool] *W*; are fool *Q1–3*.

---

　16. *fubbs*] a small chubby person (a term of endearment).
　17. *pug*] monkey or other small animal; imp; courtesan.

ANTONIO.

Home, Madonna!

AQUILINA.

Ay home, sir. Who am I?   25

ANTONIO.

Madonna, as I take it you are my—you are—thou art my
little Nicky Nacky—that's all!

AQUILINA.

I find you are resolved to be troublesome, and so to make
short of the matter in few words, I hate you, detest you,
loath you, I am weary of you, sick of you—hang you, you   30
are an old, silly, impertinent, impotent, solicitous coxcomb,
crazy in your head, and lazy in your body, love to be
meddling with everything, and if you had not money, you
are good for nothing.

ANTONIO.

Good for nothing! Hurry durry, I'll try that presently.   35
Sixty-one years old, and good for nothing; that's brave.
(*To the* Maid.)   Come come come Mistress Fiddle-faddle,
turn you out for a season. Go turn out I say, it is our will and
pleasure to be private some moments—out out when you
are bid to—   *Puts her out and locks the door.* 40
Good for nothing you say?

AQUILINA.

Why, what are you good for?

ANTONIO.

In the first place, madam, I am old, and consequently very
wise, very wise, Madonna, d'e mark that? In the second
place take notice, if you please, that I am a Senator, and   45
when I think fit can make speeches, Madonna. Hurry
durry, I can make a speech in the Senate-house now and
then would make your hair stand on end, Madonna.

AQUILINA.

What care I for your speeches in the Senate-house? If you
would be silent here I should thank you.   50

ANTONIO.

Why, I can make speeches to thee too, my lovely Madonna;
for example—
My cruel fair one,

          Takes out a purse of gold, and at every pause shakes it.

Since it is my fate, that you should with
Your servant angry prove; though late at night—   55
I hope 'tis not too late with this to gain
Reception for my love—
There's for thee, my little Nicky Nacky—take it, here take
it—I say take it, or I'll throw it at your head—how now,
rebel!   60

AQUILINA.

Truly, my illustrious Senator, I must confess your Honor is
at present most profoundly eloquent indeed.

ANTONIO.

Very well. Come, now let's sit down and think upon't a
little—come sit I say—sit down by me a little, my Nicky
Nacky, hah—(*Sits down.*) Hurry durry—good for noth-   65
ing—

AQUILINA.

No sir, if you please, I can know my distance and stand.

ANTONIO.

Stand! How? Nacky up and I down! Nay then, let me
exclaim with the poet:

Show me a case more pitiful who can,   70
A standing woman, and a falling man.

Hurry durry—not sit down—"see this ye Gods." You won't
sit down?

AQUILINA.

No sir.

ANTONIO.

Then look you now, suppose me a bull, a Basan-bull, the   75
bull of bulls, or any bull. Thus up I get and with my brows
thus bent—I broo, I say I broo, I broo, I broo. You won't
sit down will you?—I broo—

Bellows like a bull, and drives her about.

AQUILINA.

Well, sir, I must endure this.   *She sits down.*
Now your Honor has been a bull, pray what beast will your   80
Worship please to be next?

ANTONIO.

Now I'll be a Senator again, and thy lover, little Nicky

---

75. *Basan-bull*] see Psalms 22:12.

Nacky! (*He sits by her.*) Ah toad, toad, toad, toad! Spit in my face a little, Nacky—spit in my face, prithee, spit in my face never so little; spit but a little bit—spit, spit, spit, 85 spit when you are bid I say! Do, prithee spit—now, now, now, spit. What, you won't spit, will you? Then I'll be a dog.

AQUILINA.

A dog, my lord?

ANTONIO.

Ay, a dog—and I'll give thee this t'other purse to let me be 90 a dog—and to use me like a dog a little. Hurry durry—I will—here 'tis.— *Gives the purse.*

AQUILINA.

Well, with all my heart. But let me beseech your Dogship to play your tricks over as fast as you can, that you may come to stinking the sooner, and be turned out of doors as 95 you deserve.

ANTONIO.

Ay, ay. No matter for that. (*He gets under the table.*) That shan't move me. Now, bough waugh waugh, bough waugh— *Barks like a dog.*

AQUILINA.

Hold, hold, hold sir, I beseech you. What is't you do? If curs bite, they must be kicked, sir. Do you see, kicked 100 thus.

ANTONIO,

Ay, with all my heart. Do kick, kick on, now I am under the table, kick again—kick harder—harder yet, bough waugh waugh, waugh, bough—'odd, I'll have a snap at thy shins—bough waugh waugh, waugh, bough—'odd she kicks 105 bravely.—

AQUILINA.

Nay then I'll go another way to work with you; and I think here's an instrument fit for the purpose. (*Fetches a whip and bell.*) What, bite your mistress, sirrah! Out, out of doors, you dog, to kennel and be hanged—bite your 110 mistress by the legs, you rogue?— *She whips him.*

ANTONIO.

Nay prithee, Nacky, now thou art too loving. Hurry durry, 'odd I'll be a dog no longer.

AQUILINA.

Nay, none of your fawning and grinning, but begone, or
here's the discipline. What, bite your mistress by the legs, 115
you mongrel? Out of doors—hout hout, to kennel, sirrah!
Go!

ANTONIO.

This is very barbarous usage, Nacky, very barbarous. Look
you, I will not go—I will not stir from the door, that I
resolve—hurry durry, what, shut me out?   120

She whips him out.

AQUILINA.

Ay, and if you come here any more tonight I'll have my
footmen lug you, you cur. What, bite your poor mistress
Nacky, sirrah!

Enter Maid.

MAID.

Heavens, madam! Whats the matter?

He howls at the door like a dog.

AQUILINA.

Call my footmen hither presently.   125

Enter two Footmen.

MAID.

They are here already, madam. The house is all alarmed
with a strange noise that nobody knows what to make of.

AQUILINA.

Go all of you and turn that troublesome beast in the next
room out of my house. If I ever see him within these walls
again, without my leave for his admittance, you sneaking 130
rogues—I'll have you poisoned all, poisoned, like rats.
Every corner of the house shall stink of one of you. Go, and
learn hereafter to know my pleasure. So, now for my Pierre:
Thus when godlike lover was displeased,
We sacrifice our fool and he's appeased.   135

Exeunt.

[III.ii]   *Enter* Belvidera.

BELVIDERA.

I'm sacrificed! I am sold! betrayed to shame!

–41–

Inevitable ruin has enclosed me!
No sooner was I to my bed repaired,
To weigh, and (weeping) ponder my condition,
But the old hoary wretch, to whose false care   5
My peace and honor was entrusted, came
(Like Tarquin) ghastly with infernal lust.
Oh thou Roman Lucrece!
Thou couldst find friends to vindicate thy wrong;
I never had but one, and he's proved false;   10
He that should guard my virtue has betrayed it;
Left me! undone me! Oh that I could hate him!
Where shall I go! Oh whither, whither wander?

Enter Jaffeir.

JAFFEIR.

Can Belvidera want a resting place
When these poor arms are open to receive her?   15
Oh 'tis in vain to struggle with desires
Strong as my love to thee; for every moment
I am from thy sight, the heart within my bosom
Moans like a tender infant in its cradle
Whose nurse had left it. Come, and with the songs   20
Of gentle love persuade it to its peace.

BELVIDERA.

I fear the stubborn wanderer will not own me,
'Tis grown a rebel to be ruled no longer,
Scorns the indulgent bosom that first lulled it,
And like a disobedient child disdains   25
The soft authority of Belvidera.

JAFFEIR.

There was a time—

BELVIDERA.   Yes, yes, there was a time,
When Belvidera's tears, her cries, and sorrows,
Were not despised; when if she chanced to sigh,
Or look but sad—there was indeed a time   30
When Jaffeir would have ta'en her in his arms,
Eased her declining head upon his breast,
And never left her till he found the cause.
But let her now weep seas,
Cry till she rend the earth, sigh till she burst   35

Her heart asunder; still he bears it all,
Deaf as the wind, and as the rocks unshaken.

JAFFEIR.
Have I been deaf? Am I that rock unmoved,
Against whose root tears beat, and sighs are sent
In vain? Have I beheld thy sorrows calmly?   40
Witness against me, Heav'ns, have I done this?
Then bear me in a whirlwind back again,
And let that angry dear one ne'er forgive me!
Oh thou too rashly censur'st of my love!
Couldst thou but think how I have spent this night,   45
Dark and alone, no pillow to my head,
Rest in my eyes, nor quiet in my heart,
Thou wouldst not, Belvidera, sure thou wouldst not
Talk to me thus, but like a pitying angel
Spreading thy wings come settle on my breast,   50
And hatch warm comfort there ere sorrows freeze it.

BELVIDERA.
Why then, poor mourner, in what baleful corner
Hast thou been talking with that witch the night?
On what cold stone hast thou been stretched along,
Gathering the grumbling winds about thy head,   55
To mix with theirs the accents of thy woes?
Oh now I find the cause my love forsakes me!
I am no longer fit to bear a share
In his concernments: my weak female virtue
Must not be trusted; 'tis too frail and tender.   60

JAFFEIR.
Oh Porcia! Porcia! What a soul was thine!

BELVIDERA.
That Porcia was a woman, and when Brutus,
Big with the fate of Rome (Heav'n guard thy safety!),
Concealed from her the labors of his mind,
She let him see her blood was great as his,   65
Flowed from a spring as noble, and a heart
Fit to partake his troubles, as his love.

62–65. *Porcia . . . his*] She cut her thigh to prove she could keep a secret
under torture. She was daughter of Cato Uticensis, who committed suicide
rather than yield to the tyrant Caesar.

Fetch, fetch that dagger back, the dreadful dower
Thou gav'st last night in parting with me; strike it
Here to my heart; and as the blood flows from it,   70
Judge if it run not pure as Cato's daughter's.

JAFFEIR.

Thou art too good, and I indeed unworthy,
Unworthy so much virtue. Teach me how
I may deserve such matchless love as thine,
And see with what attention I'll obey thee.   75

BELVIDERA.

Do not despise me; that's the all I ask.

JAFFEIR.

Despise thee! Hear me—

BELVIDERA.   Oh thy charming tongue
Is but too well acquainted with my weakness,
Knows, let it name but love, my melting heart
Dissolves within my breast, till with closed eyes   80
I reel into thy arms, and all's forgotten.

JAFFEIR.

What shall I do?

BELVIDERA.   Tell me! be just, and tell me
Why dwells that busy cloud upon thy face?
Why am I made a stranger? Why that sigh,
And I not know the cause? Why when the world   85
Is wrapped in rest, why chooses then my love
To wander up and down in horrid darkness,
Loathing his bed, and these desiring arms?
Why are these eyes bloodshot with tedious watching?
Why starts he now, and looks as if he wished   90
His fate were finished? Tell me, ease my fears,
Lest when we next time meet, I want the power
To search into the sickness of thy mind,
But talk as wildly then as thou look'st now.

JAFFEIR.

Oh Belvidera!   95

BELVIDERA.

Why was I last night delivered to a villain?

JAFFEIR.

Hah, a villain!

BELVIDERA.

Yes! to a villain! Why at such an hour

Meets that assembly all made up of wretches
That look as Hell had drawn 'em into league?   100
Why, I in this hand, and in that a dagger,
Was I delivered with such dreadful ceremonies?
"To you, sirs, and to your honor I bequeath her,
And with her this. Whene'er I prove unworthy,
You know the rest, then strike it to her heart."   105
Oh! why's that "rest" concealed from me? Must I
Be made the hostage of a hellish trust?
For such I know I am, that's all my value!
But by the love and loyalty I owe thee,
I'll free thee from the bondage of these slaves;   110
Straight to the Senate, tell 'em all I know,
All that I think, all that my fears inform me!

JAFFEIR.
Is this the Roman virtue! this the blood
That boasts its purity with Cato's daughter!
Would she have e'er betrayed her Brutus?   No: 115

BELVIDERA.
For Brutus trusted her. Wert thou so kind,
What would not Belvidera suffer for thee?

JAFFEIR.
I shall undo myself, and tell thee all.

BELVIDERA.
Look not upon me as I am, a woman,
But as a bone, thy wife, thy friend, who long   120
Has had admission to thy heart, and there
Studied the virtues of thy gallant nature;
Thy constancy, thy courage and thy truth,
Have been my daily lesson. I have learnt them,
Am bold as thou, can suffer or despise   125
The worst of fates for thee, and with thee share them.

JAFFEIR.
Oh you divinest Powers! look down and hear
My prayers! Instruct me to reward this virtue!
Yet think a little, ere thou tempt me further;
Think I have a tale to tell, will shake thy nature,   130
Melt all this boasted constancy thou talk'st of
Into vile tears and despicable sorrows—
Then if thou shouldst betray me!

BELVIDERA.   Shall I swear?

JAFFEIR.

    No. Do not swear. I would not violate
    Thy tender nature with so rude a bond.   135
    But as thou hop'st to see me live my days,
    And love thee long, lock this within thy breast;
    I've bound myself by all the strictest sacraments,
    Divine and human—

BELVIDERA.   Speak!—

JAFFEIR.   To kill thy father—

BELVIDERA.

    My father!

JAFFEIR.   Nay, the throats of the whole Senate   140
    Shall bleed, my Belvidera. He amongst us
    That spares his father, brother, or his friend,
    Is damned. How rich and beauteous will the face
    Of ruin look when these wide streets run blood;
    I and the glorious partners of my fortune   145
    Shouting, and striding o'er the prostrate dead,
    Still to new waste; whilst thou, far off in safety
    Smiling, shalt see the wonders of our daring,
    And when night comes, with praise and love receive me.

BELVIDERA.

    Oh!

JAFFEIR. Have a care, and shrink not even in thought!   150
    For if thou dost—

BELVIDERA.   I know it, thou wilt kill me.
    Do, strike thy sword into this bosom; lay me
    Dead on the earth, and then thou wilt be safe.
    Murder my father! Though his cruel nature
    Has persecuted me to my undoing,   155
    Driven me to basest wants, can I behold him
    With smiles of vengeance, butchered in his age?
    The sacred fountain of my life destroyed?
    And canst thou shed the blood that gave me being?
    Nay, be a traitor too, and sell thy country;   160
    Can thy great heart descend so vilely low,
    Mix with hired slaves, bravoes, and common stabbers,
    Nose-slitters, alley-lurking villains! join
    With such a crew, and take a ruffian's wages,
    To cut the throats of wretches as they sleep?   165

JAFFEIR.

    Thou wrong'st me, Belvidera! I've engaged
    With men of souls, fit to reform the ills
    Of all mankind. There's not a heart amongst them,
    But's as stout as death, yet honest as the nature
    Of man first made, ere fraud and vice were fashions.   170

BELVIDERA.

    What's he, to whose cursed hands last night thou gav'st me?
    Was that well done? Oh! I could tell a story
    Would rouse thy lion heart out of its den,
    And make it rage with terrifying fury.

JAFFEIR.

    Speak on I charge thee!

BELVIDERA.   Oh my love! if ere   175
    Thy Belvidera's peace deserved thy care,
    Remove me from this place. Last night, last night!

JAFFEIR.

    Distract me not, but give me all the truth.

BELVIDERA.

    No sooner wert thou gone, and I alone,
    Left in the pow'r of that old son of mischief;   180
    No sooner was I lain on my sad bed,
    But that vile wretch approached me, loose, unbuttoned,
    Ready for violation. Then my heart
    Throbbed with its fears; oh how I wept and sighed,
    And shrunk and trembled; wished in vain for him   185
    That should protect me. Thou alas! wert gone!

JAFFEIR.

    Patience, sweet Heav'n! till I make vengeance sure.

BELVIDERA.

    He drew the hideous dagger forth thou gav'st him,
    And with upbraiding smiles he said, "Behold it;
    This is the pledge of a false husband's love!"   190
    And in my arms then pressed, and would have clasped me;
    But with my cries I scared his coward heart,
    Till he withdrew, and muttered vows to Hell.
    These are thy friends! With these thy life, thy honor,
    Thy love, all's staked, and all will go to ruin.   195

JAFFEIR.

    No more! I charge thee keep this secret close;

Clear up thy sorrows, look as if thy wrongs
Were all forgot, and treat him like a friend,
As no complaint were made. No more, retire,
Retire my life, and doubt not of my honor;   200
I'll heal its failings, and deserve thy love.

BELVIDERA.

Oh should I part with thee, I fear thou wilt
In anger leave me, and return no more.

JAFFEIR.

Return no more! I would not live without thee
Another night to purchase the creation.   205

BELVIDERA.

When shall we meet again?

JAFFEIR.   Anon at twelve!
I'll steal myself to thy expecting arms,
Come like a traveled dove and bring thee peace.

BELVIDERA.

Indeed?

JAFFEIR.   By all our loves!

BELVIDERA.   'Tis hard to part;
But sure no falsehood e'er looked so fairly.   210
Farewell—remember twelve.   *Exit* Belvidera.

JAFFEIR.   Let Heav'n forget me
When I remember not thy truth, thy love.
How cursed is my condition, tossed and jostled
From every corner; fortune's common fool,
The jest of rogues, an instrumental ass   215
For villains to lay loads of shame upon,
And drive about just for their ease and scorn.

Enter Pierre.

PIERRE.

Jaffeir!

JAFFEIR.   Who calls?

PIERRE.   A friend, that could have wished
T'have found thee otherwise employed. What, hunt
A wife on the dull foil! Sure a staunch husband   220
Of all hounds is the dullest? Wilt thou never,

---

220. *foil*] the track of a hunted animal.

Never be weaned from caudles and confections?
What feminine tale hast thou been listening to,
Of unaired shirts, catarrhs and toothache got
By thin-soled shoes? Damnation! that a fellow   225
Chosen to be a sharer in the destruction
Of a whole people, should sneak thus in corners
To ease his fulsome lusts, and fool his mind.

JAFFEIR.
May not a man then trifle out an hour
With a kind woman and not wrong his calling?   230

PIERRE.
Not in a cause like ours.

JAFFEIR.   Then, friend, our cause
Is in a damned condition: for I'll tell thee,
That canker-worm called lechery has touched it,
'Tis tainted vilely. Wouldst thou think it, Renault
(That mortified old withered winter rogue),   235
Loves simple fornication like a priest.
I found him out for watering at my wife;
He visited her last night like a kind guardian.
Faith, she has some temptations, that's the truth on't.

PIERRE.
He durst not wrong his trust!

JAFFEIR.   'Twas something late though 240
To take the freedom of a lady's chamber.

PIERRE.
Was she in bed?

JAFFEIR.   Yes faith, in virgin sheets
White as her bosom, Pierre, dished neatly up,
Might tempt a weaker appetite to taste.
Oh how the old fox stunk, I warrant thee,   245
When the rank fit was on him.

PIERRE.   Patience guide me!
He used no violence?

JAFFEIR.   No, no! out on't, violence!
Played with her neck; brushed her with his grey-beard,
Struggled and toused, tickled her till she squeaked a little
May be, or so—but not a jot of violence—   250

---

222. *caudles and confections*] warm drinks and sugary medicines.

PIERRE.

    Damn him.

JAFFEIR.   Ay, so say I. But hush, no more on't;
    All hitherto is well, and I believe
    Myself no monster yet, though no man knows
    What fate he's born to. Sure 'tis near the hour
    We all should meet for our concluding orders.   255
    Will the ambassador be here in person?

PIERRE.

    No. He has sent commission to that villain, Renault,
    To give the executing charge.
    I'd have thee be a man if possible
    And keep thy temper, for a brave revenge   260
    Ne'er comes too late.

JAFFEIR.   Fear not, I am cool as Patience.
    Had he completed my dishonor, rather
    Than hazard the success our hopes are ripe for,
    I'd bear it all with mortifying virtue.

PIERRE.

    He's yonder coming this way through the hall;   265
    His thoughts seem full.

JAFFEIR.   Prithee retire, and leave me
    With him alone. I'll put him to some trial,
    See how his rotten part will bear the touching.

PIERRE.

    Be careful then.   *Exit* Pierre.

JAFFEIR.   Nay, never doubt, but trust me.
    What, be a devil! Take a damning oath   270
    For shedding native blood! Can there be a sin
    In merciful repentance? Oh this villain!

Enter Renault.

RENAULT.

    Perverse! and peevish! what a slave is Man!
    To let his itching flesh thus get the better of him!
    Dispatch the tool her husband—that were well.   275
    Who's there?

JAFFEIR.   A man.

---

253. *monster*] cuckold.

RENAULT.   My friend, my near ally!
    The hostage of your faith, my beauteous charge,
    Is very well.
JAFFEIR.   Sir, are you sure of that?
    Stands she in perfect health? Beats her pulse even?
    Neither too hot nor cold?
RENAULT.   What means that question?   280
JAFFEIR.
    Oh, women have fantastic constitutions,
    Inconstant as their wishes, always wavering,
    And ne'er fixed. Was it not boldly done
    Even at first sight to trust the thing I loved
    (A tempting treasure too!) with youth so fierce   285
    And vigorous as thine? But thou art honest.
RENAULT.
    Who dares accuse me?
JAFFEIR.   Cursed be him that doubts
    Thy virtue! I have tried it, and declare,
    Were I to choose a guardian of my honor
    I'd put it into thy keeping: for I know thee.   290
RENAULT.
    Know me!
JAFFEIR.   Ay, know thee: there's no falsehood in thee.
    Thou look'st just as thou art. Let us embrace.
    Now wouldst thou cut my throat or I cut thine?
RENAULT.
    You dare not do't.
JAFFEIR.   You lie, sir.
RENAULT.   How!
JAFFEIR.   No more.
    'Tis a base world, and must reform, that's all.   295

Enter Spinosa, Theodore, Eliot, Revellido, Durand, Brainveil, *and the
rest of the* Conspirators.

RENAULT.
    Spinosa! Theodore!
SPINOSA.   The same.
RENAULT.   You are welcome!
SPINOSA.
    You are trembling, sir.

RENAULT. 'Tis a cold night indeed. I am aged,
Full of decay and natural infirmities.

Pierre *re-enters.*

We shall be warm, my friend, I hope tomorrow.
PIERRE [*to* Jaffeir].
'Twas not well done: thou shouldst have stroked him   300
And not have galled him.
JAFFEIR [*to* Pierre].   Damn him, let him chew on't.
Heav'n! where am I? Beset with cursed fiends,
That wait to damn me; what a devil's Man,
When he forgets his nature—hush my heart.
RENAULT.
My friends, 'tis late. Are we assembled all?   305
Where's Theodore?
THEODORE.   At hand.
RENAULT.   Spinosa.
SPINOSA.   Here.
RENAULT.
Brainveil.
BRAINVEIL.   I am ready.
RENAULT.   Durand and Brabe.
DURAND.   Command us,
We are both prepared!
RENAULT.   Mezzana, Revellido,
Ternon, Retrosi; oh you are men I find
Fit to behold your fate, and meet her summons.   310
Tomorrow's rising sun must see you all
Decked in your honors! Are the soldiers ready?
OMNES.
All, all.
RENAULT.
You, Durand, with your thousand must possess
St. Marks; you, captain, know your charge already;   315
'Tis to secure the ducal palace; you,
Brabe, with a hundred more must gain the Secque.
With the like number Brainveil to the Procuralle.

---

317. *Secque*] the Mint.
318. *Procuralle*] the residence of the Procurators, the highest officials in
the republic after the Doge.

Be all this done with the least tumult possible,
Till in each place you post sufficient guards: 320
Then sheath your swords in every breast you meet.

JAFFEIR.
Oh reverend cruelty; damned bloody villain!

RENAULT.
During this execution, Durand, you
Must in the midst keep your battalia fast,
And Theodore, be sure to plant the cannon   325
That may command the streets; whilst Revellido,
Mezzana, Ternon, and Retrosi guard you.
(This done!) we'll give the general alarm,
Apply petards, and force the Ars'nal gates;
Then fire the city round in several places,   330
Or with our cannon (if it dare resist)
Batter't to ruin. But above all, I charge you
Shed blood enough, spare neither sex nor age,
Name nor condition; if there live a Senator
After tomorrow, though the dullest rogue   335
That e'er said nothing, we have lost our ends.
If possible, let's kill the very name
Of Senator, and bury it in blood.

JAFFEIR.
Merciless, horrid slave!—Ay, blood enough!
Shed blood enough, old Renault. How thou charm'st me! 340

RENAULT.
But one thing more, and then farewell till fate
Join us again, or separate us ever:
First, let's embrace. Heav'n knows who next shall thus
Wing ye together. But let's all remember
We wear no common cause upon our swords;   345
Let each man think that on his single virtue
Depends the good and fame of all the rest,
Eternal honor or perpetual infamy.
Let's remember, through what dreadful hazards
Propitious fortune hitherto has led us,   350
How often on the brink of some discovery
Have we stood tottering, and yet still kept our ground
So well, the busiest searchers ne'er could follow
Those subtle tracks which puzzled all suspicion—
You droop, sir.

JAFFEIR.   No. With a most profound attention   355
    I've heard it all, and wonder at thy virtue.
RENAULT.
    Though there be yet few hours 'twixt them and ruin,
    Are not the Senate lulled in full security,
    Quiet and satisfied, as fools are always!
    Never did so profound repose forerun   360
    Calamity so great. Nay, our good fortune
    Has blinded the most piercing of mankind,
    Strengthened the fearfull'st, charmed the most suspectful,
    Confounded the most subtle: for we live,
    We live, my friends, and quickly shall our life   365
    Prove fatal to these tyrants. Let's consider
    That we destroy oppression, avarice,
    A people nursed up equally with vices
    And loathsome lusts, which Nature most abhors,
    And such as without shame she cannot suffer.   370
JAFFEIR.
    Oh Belvidera, take me to thy arms
    And show me where's my peace, for I've lost it.   *Exit* Jaffeir.
RENAULT.
    Without the least remorse then let's resolve
    With fire and sword t'exterminate these tyrants,
    And when we shall behold those cursed tribunals,   375
    Stained by the tears and sufferings of the innocent,
    Burning with flames rather from Heav'n than ours,
    The raging furious and unpitying soldier
    Pulling his reeking dagger from the bosoms
    Of gasping wretches, death in every quarter,   380
    With all that sad disorder can produce
    To make a spectacle of horror: then,
    Then let's call to mind, my dearest friends,
    That there's nothing pure upon the earth,
    That the most valued things have most alloys,   385
    And that in change of all those vile enormities,
    Under whose weight this wretched country labors,
    The means are only in our hands to crown them.
PIERRE.
    And may those powers above that are propitious
    To gallant minds record this cause, and bless it.   390

RENAULT.

    Thus happy, thus secure of all we wish for,
    Should there, my friends, be found amongst us one
    False to this glorious enterprise, what fate,
    What vengeance were enough for such a villain?

ELIOT.

    Death here without repentance, Hell hereafter.   395

RENAULT.

    Let that be my lot, if as here I stand
    'Listed by fate amongst her darling sons,
    Though I had one only brother, dear by all
    The strictest ties of nature; though one hour
    Had given us birth, one fortune fed our wants,   400
    One only love, and that but of each other,
    Still filled our minds; could I have such a friend
    Joined in this cause, and had but ground to fear
    Meant foul play, may this right hand drop from me,
    If I'd not hazard all my future peace,   405
    And stab him to the heart before you. Who
    Would do less? Wouldst not thou, Pierre, the same?

PIERRE.

    You have singled me, sir, out for this hard question,
    As if 'twere started only for my sake!
    Am I the thing you fear? Here, here's my bosom,   410
    Search it with all your swords! Am I a traitor?

RENAULT.

    No. But I fear your late commended friend
    Is little less. Come sirs, 'tis now no time
    To trifle with our safety. Where's this Jaffeir?

SPINOSA.

    He left the room just now in strange disorder.   415

RENAULT.

    Nay, there is danger in him. I observed him,
    During the time I took for explanation,
    He was transported from most deep attention
    To a confusion which he could not smother.
    His looks grew full of sadness and surprise,   420

407. Would do] *Q3, W*; Would
not do *Q1–2*.

All which betrayed a wavering spirit in him
That labored with reluctancy and sorrow.
What's requisite for safety must be done
With speedy execution; he remains
Yet in our power. I for my own part wear   425
A dagger.

PIERRE.   Well?

RENAULT.   And I could wish it—

PIERRE.   Where?

RENAULT.

Buried in his heart.

PIERRE.   Away! W'are yet all friends;
No more of this, 'twill breed ill blood amongst us.

SPINOSA.

Let us all draw our swords, and search the house,
Pull him from the dark hole where he sits brooding   430
O'er his cold fears, and each man kill his share of him.

PIERRE.

Who talks of killing? Who's he'll shed the blood
That's dear to me? Is't you? or you? or you, sir?
What, not one speak? How you stand gaping all
On your grave oracle, your wooden god there;   435
Yet not a word? (*to* Renault) Then, sir, I'll tell you a secret,
Suspicion's but at best a coward's virtue!

RENAULT.

A coward—   *Handles his sword.*

PIERRE.   Put, put up thy sword, old man,
Thy hand shakes at it; come, let's heal this breach.
I am too hot; we yet may live friends.   440

SPINOSA.

Till we are safe, our friendship cannot be so.

PIERRE.

Again! Who's that?

SPINOSA.   'Twas I.

THEODORE.   And I.

REVELLIDO.   And I.

ELIOT.

And all.

RENAULT.

Who are on my side?

SPINOSA. Every honest sword.
Let's die like men and not be sold like slaves. 445
PIERRE.
One such word more, by Heav'n I'll to the Senate
And hang ye all, like dogs in clusters!
Why peep your coward swords half out their shells?
Why do you not all brandish them like mine?
You fear to die, and yet dare talk of killing? 450
RENAULT.
Go to the Senate and betray us; hasten,
Secure thy wretched life; we fear to die
Less than thou dar'st be honest.
PIERRE. That's rank falsehood.
Fear'st not thou death? Fie, there's a knavish itch
In that salt blood, an utter foe to smarting. 455
Had Jaffeir's wife proved kind, he had still been true.
Foh—how that stinks?
Thou die! Thou kill my friend! or thou, or thou,
Or thou, with that lean withered wretched face!
Away! Disperse all to your several charges, 460
And meet tomorrow where your honor calls you.
I'll bring that man, whose blood you so much thirst for,
And you shall see him venture for you fairly—
Hence, hence, I say. *Exit* Renault *angrily.*
SPONOSA. I fear we have been too blame,
And done too much. 465
THEODORE.
'Twas too far urged against the man you loved.
REVELLIDO.
Here, take our swords and crush 'em with your feet.
SPINOSA.
Forgive us, gallant friend.
PIERRE. Nay, now y'have found
The way to melt and cast me as you will:
I'll fetch this friend and give him to your mercy. 470

464. too blame] *Q1*; to blame
Q2–3, W.

---

464. *too blame*] too blameworthy, "a characteristic usage of the 16th–17th
centuries" (G).

Nay, he shall die if you will take him from me.
For your repose I'll quit my heart's jewel,
But would not have him torn away by villains
And spiteful villainy.

SPINOSA.   No. May you both
Forever live and fill the world with fame!   475

PIERRE.
Now you are too kind. Whence rose all this discord?
Oh what a dangerous precipice have we 'scaped!
How near a fall was all we had long been building!
What an eternal blot had stained our glories,
If one the bravest and the best of men   480
Had fallen a sacrifice to rash suspicion,
Butchered by those whose cause he came to cherish!
Oh could you know him all as I have known him,
How good he is, how just, how true, how brave,
You would not leave this place till you had seen him,   485
Humbled yourselves before him, kissed his feet,
And gained remission for the worst of follies.
    Come but tomorrow all your doubts shall end,
    And to your loves me better recommend,
    That I've preserved your fame, and saved my friend.   490

Exeunt omnes.

ACT IV

Enter Jaffeir *and* Belvidera.

JAFFEIR.

    Where dost thou lead me? Every step I move,
    Methinks I tread upon some mangled limb
    Of a racked friend. Oh my dear charming ruin!
    Where are we wand'ring?

BELVIDERA.   To eternal honor;
    To do a deed shall chronicle thy name   5
    Among the glorious legends of those few
    That have saved sinking nations. Thy renown
    Shall be the future song of all the virgins,
    Who by thy piety have been preserved
    From horrid violation; every street   10
    Shall be adorned with statues to thy honor,
    And at thy feet this great inscription written,
    "Remember him that propped the fall of Venice."

JAFFEIR.

    Rather, remember him, who after all
    The sacred bonds of oaths and holier friendship,   15
    In fond compassion to a woman's tears
    Forgot his manhood, virtue, truth, and honor,
    To sacrifice the bosom that relieved him.
    Why wilt thou damn me?

BELVIDERA.   Oh inconstant man!
    How will you promise? How will you deceive?   20
    Do, return back, replace me in my bondage,
    Tell all thy friends how dangerously thou lov'st me;
    And let thy dagger do its bloody office.
    Oh that kind dagger, Jaffeir, how 'twill look
    Stuck through my heart, drenched in my blood to th' hilts!   25
    Whilst these poor dying eyes shall with their tears
    No more torment thee; then thou wilt be free.
    Or if thou think'st it nobler, let me live
    Till I am a victim to the hateful lust
    Of that infernal devil, that old fiend   30

That's damned himself and would undo mankind.
Last night, my love!
JAFFEIR.   Name, name it not again.
    It shows a beastly image to my fancy
    Will wake me into madness. Oh the villain!
    That durst approach such purity as thine   35
    On terms so vile. Destruction, swift destruction
    Fall on my coward head, and make my name
    The common scorn of fools if I forgive him.
    If I forgive him! If I not revenge
    With utmost rage, and most unstaying fury   40
    Thy sufferings, thou dear darling of my life, love.
BELVIDERA.
    Delay no longer then, but to the Senate;
    And tell the dismal'st story e'er was uttered;
    Tell 'em what bloodshed, rapines, desolations,
    Have been prepared, how near's the fatal hour!   45
    Save thy poor country, save the reverend blood
    Of all its nobles, which tomorrow's dawn
    Must else see shed; save the poor tender lives
    Of all those little infants which the swords
    Of murderers are whetting for this moment.   50
    Think thou already hear'st their dying screams,
    Think that thou seest their sad distracted mothers
    Kneeling before thy feet, and begging pity
    With torn dishevelled hair and streaming eyes,
    Their naked mangled breasts besmeared with blood,   55
    And even the milk with which their fondled babes
    Softly they hushed, dropping in anguish from 'em.
    Think thou seest this, and then consult thy heart.
JAFFEIR.
    Oh!
BELVIDERA.
    Think too, if thou lose this present minute,
    What miseries the next day bring upon thee.   60
    Imagine all the horrors of that night,
    Murder and rapine, waste and desolation,
    Confusedly ranging. Think what then may prove
    My lot! The ravisher may then come safe,
    And midst the terror of the public ruin   65

Do a damned deed; perhaps too lay a train
May catch thy life. Then where will be revenge,
The dear revenge that's due to such a wrong?

JAFFEIR.

By all Heaven's powers, prophetic truth dwells in thee,
For every word thou speak'st strikes through my heart   70
Like a new light, and shows it how't has wandered.
Just what th' hast made me, take me, Belvidera.
And lead me to the place where I'm to say
This bitter lesson, where I must betray
My truth, my virtue, constancy and friends.   75
Must I betray my friends? Ah take me quickly,
Secure me well before that thought's renewed:
If I relapse once more, all's lost forever.

BELVIDERA.

Hast thou a friend more dear than Belvidera?

JAFFEIR.

No, th'art my soul itself; wealth, friendship, honor,   80
All present joys, and earnest of all future,
Are summed in thee. Methinks when in thy arms
Thus leaning on thy breast, one minute's more
Than a long thousand years of vulgar hours.
Why was such happiness not given me pure?   85
Why dashed with cruel wrongs, and bitter wantings?
Come, lead me forward now like a tame lamb
To sacrifice. Thus in his fatal garlands,
Decked fine and pleased, the wanton skips and plays,
    Trots by the enticing flattering priestess' side,   90
    And much transported with his little pride,
    Forgets his dear companions of the plain,
    Till by her, bound, he's on the altar lain;
    Yet then too hardly bleats, such pleasure's in the pain.

Enter Officer *and six* Guards.

OFFICER.

Stand! Who goes there?   95

BELVIDERA.

Friends.

66. perhaps too] *G*; perhaps to
Q1-3; perhaps may *W*.

JAFFEIR.

    Friends, Belvidera! hide me from my friends.
    By Heaven I'd rather see the face of Hell,
    Than meet the man I love.

OFFICER.   But what friends are you?

BELVIDERA.

    Friends to the Senate and the State of Venice.   100

OFFICER.

    My orders are to seize on all I find
    At this late hour, and bring 'em to the Council,
    Who now are sitting.

JAFFEIR.   Sir, you shall be obeyed.

    Hold, brutes, stand off, none of your paws upon me.
    Now the lot's cast, and fate do what thou wilt.   105

                                Exeunt guarded.

[IV.ii]   *Scene, The Senate House.*

Where appear sitting, the Duke of Venice, Priuli, Antonio, *and eight other* Senators.

DUKE.

    Antonio, Priuli, Senators of Venice,
    Speak. Why are we assembled here this night?
    What have you to inform us of concerns
    The State of Venice, honor, or its safety?

PRIULI.

    Could words express the story I have to tell you,   5
    Fathers, these tears were useless, these sad tears
    That fall from my old eyes; but there is cause
    We all should weep, tear off these purple robes,
    And wrap ourselves in sackcloth, sitting down
    On the sad earth, and cry aloud to Heaven.   10
    Heaven knows if yet there be an hour to come
    Ere Venice be no more!

ALL SENATORS.   How!

PRIULI.   Nay, we stand

    Upon the very brink of gaping ruin.
    Within this city's formed a dark conspiracy
    To massacre us all, our wives and children,   15

Kindred and friends, our palaces and temples
To lay in ashes; nay the hour too, fixed,
The swords, for aught I know, drawn even this moment,
And the wild waste begun. From unknown hands
I had this warning. But if we are men   20
Let's not be tamely butchered, but do something
That may inform the world in after ages,
Our virtue was not ruined though we were.

A NOISE WITHOUT.

Room, room, make room for some prisoners—

SENATOR.

Let's raise the city.

Enter Officer *and* Guard.

PRIULI.   Speak there, what disturbance?   25

OFFICER.

Two prisoners have the guard seized in the streets,
Who say they come to inform this reverend Senate
About the present danger.

Enter Jaffeir *and* Belvidera *guarded.*

ALL.   Give 'em entrance—

Well, who are you?

JAFFEIR.   A villain.

ANTONIO.   Short and pithy.

The man speaks well.

JAFFEIR.   Would every man that hears me   30
Would deal so honestly, and own his title.

DUKE.

'Tis rumored that a plot has been contrived
Against this state; that you have a share in't too.
If you are a villain, to redeem your honor,
Unfold the truth and be restored with mercy.   35

JAFFEIR.

Think not that I to save my life come hither,
I know its value better; but in pity
To all those wretches whose unhappy dooms
Are fixed and sealed. You see me here before you,
The sworn and covenanted foe of Venice.   40

–63–

But use me as my dealings may deserve
And I may prove a friend.

DUKE.   The slave capitulates.
Give him the tortures.

JAFFEIR.   That you dare not do,
Your fears won't let you, nor the longing itch
To hear a story which you dread the truth of: 45
Truth which the fear of smart shall ne'er get from me.
Cowards are scared with threat'nings, boys are whipped
Into confessions; but a steady mind
Acts of itself, ne'er asks the body counsel.
Give him the tortures! Name but such a thing   50
Again; by Heaven I'll shut these lips forever,
Not all your racks, your engines or your wheels
Shall force a groan away—that you may guess at.

ANTONIO.
A bloody minded fellow, I'll warrant;
A damned bloody minded fellow.   ,   55

DUKE.
Name your conditions.

JAFFEIR.   For myself full pardon,
Besides the lives of two and twenty friends   *Delivers a list.*
Whose names are here enrolled. Nay, let their crimes
Be ne'er so monstrous, I must have the oaths
And sacred promise of this reverend Council,   60
That in a full assembly of the Senate
The thing I ask be ratified. Swear this,
And I'll unfold the secrets of your danger.

ALL.
We'll swear.

DUKE.   Propose the oath.

JAFFEIR.   By all the hopes
Ye have of peace and happiness hereafter,   65
Swear.

ALL.   We all swear.

JAFFEIR.   To grant me what I've asked,
Ye swear.

ALL.   We swear.

46. which] *Q 3, W*; with *Q 1–2.*

JAFFEIR.   And as ye keep the oath,
May you and your posterity be blessed,
Or cursed forever.

ALL.   Else be cursed forever.

JAFFEIR.
    Then here's the list, and with't the full disclose   70
    Of all that threatens you.   *Delivers another paper.*
    Now fate, thou hast caught me.

ANTONIO.
    Why what a dreadful catalogue of cutthroats is here! I'll
    warrant you not one of these fellows but has a face like a
    lion. I dare not so much as read their names over.   75

DUKE.
    Give orders that all diligent search be made
    To seize these men. Their characters are public.
    The paper intimates their rendezvous
    To be at the house of a famed Grecian courtesan
    Called Aquilina; see that place secured.   80

ANTONIO.
    What, my Nicky Nacky, hurry durry, Nicky Nacky in the
    plot—I'll make a speech. Most noble Senators,
    What headlong apprehension drives you on,
    Right noble, wise, and truly solid Senators,
    To violate the laws and right of nations?   85
    The lady is a lady of renown.
    'Tis true, she holds a house of fair reception,
    And though I say't myself, as many more
    Can say as well as I.

SENATOR.   My lord, long speeches
    Are frivolous here, when dangers are so near us;   90
    We all well know your interest in that lady,
    The world talks loud on't.

ANTONIO.   Verily, I have done,
    I say no more.

DUKE.   But since he has declared
    Himself concerned, pray, captain, take great caution
    To treat the fair one as becomes her character,   95
    And let her bedchamber be searched with decency.
    You, Jaffeir, must with patience bear till morning,
    To be our prisoner.

JAFFEIR.   Would the chains of death
    Had bound me fast ere I had known this minute!
    I've done a deed will make my story hereafter   100
    Quoted in competition with all ill ones;
    The history of my wickedness shall run
    Down through the low traditions of the vulgar,
    And boys be taught to tell the tale of Jaffeir.

DUKE.
    Captain, withdraw your prisoner.

JAFFEIR.   Sir, if possible,   105
    Lead me where my own thoughts themselves may lose me,
    Where I may doze out what I've left of life,
    Forget myself and this day's guilt and falsehood.
    Cruel remembrance, how shall I appease thee!   *Exit guarded.*

NOISE WITHOUT.
    More traitors; room, room, make room there.   110

DUKE.
    How's this, guards?
    Where are our guards? Shut up the gates, the treason's
    Already at our doors.

                 Enter Officer.

OFFICER.   My lords, more traitors:
    Seized in the very act of consultation;
    Furnished with arms and instruments of mischief.   115
    Bring in the prisoners.

Enter Pierre, Renault, Theodore, Eliot, Revellido *and other* conspira-
                tors, *in fetters, guarded.*

PIERRE.   You, my Lords and Fathers,
    (As you are pleased to call yourselves) of Venice;
    If you sit here to guide the course of justice,
    Why these disgraceful chains upon the limbs
    That have so often labored in your service?   120
    Are these the wreaths of triumphs ye bestow
    On those that bring you conquests home and honors?

DUKE.
    Go on, you shall be heard, sir.

104. taught] *Q3, W*; thought *Q1–2.*

ANTONIO.

And be hanged too, I hope.

PIERRE.

Are these the trophies I've deserved for fighting   125
Your battles with confederated powers,
When winds and seas conspired to overthrow you,
And brought the fleets of Spain to your own harbors?
When you, great Duke, shrunk trembling in your palace,
And saw your wife, th'Adriatic, ploughed   130
Like a lewd whore by bolder prows than yours,
Stepped not I forth, and taught your loose Venetians
The task of honor and the way to greatness;
Raised you from your capitulating fears
To stipulate the terms of sued-for peace—   135
And this my recompense? If I am a traitor
Produce my charge; or show the wretch that's base enough
And brave enough to tell me I am a traitor.

DUKE.

Know you one Jaffeir?   *All the conspirators murmur.*

PIERRE.

                          Yes, and know his virtue.
His justice, truth, his general worth and sufferings   140
From a hard father taught me first to love him.

                  Enter Jaffeir *guarded.*

DUKE.

See him brought forth.

PIERRE.   My friend too bound? Nay then,
Our fate has conquered us, and we must fall.
Why droops the man whose welfare's so much mine
They're but one thing? These reverend tyrants, Jaffeir,   145
Call us all traitors. Art thou one, my brother?

JAFFEIR.

To thee I am the falsest, veriest slave
That e'er betrayed a generous trusting friend,
And gave up honor to be sure of ruin.
All our fair hopes which morning was to have crowned   150
Has this cursed tongue o'erthrown.

PIERRE.   So, then all's over:
Venice has lost her freedom, I my life.

No more, farewell.

DUKE.   Say, will you make confession
Of your vile deeds and trust the Senate's mercy?

PIERRE.

Cursed be your Senate! Cursed your constitution!   155
The curse of growing factions and division
Still vex your councils, shake your public safety,
And make the robes of government you wear
Hateful to you, as these base chains to me.

DUKE.

Pardon or death?

PIERRE.   Death, honorable death.   160

RENAULT.

Death's the best thing we ask or you can give.

ALL CONSPIRATORS.

No shameful bonds, but honorable death!

DUKE.

Break up the Council. Captain, guard your prisoners.
Jaffeir, y'are free, but these must wait for judgment.
                        Exeunt all the Senators [*and* Belvidera].

PIERRE.

Come, where's my dungeon? Lead me to my straw.   165
It will not be the first time I've lodged hard
To do your Senate service.

JAFFEIR.   Hold one moment.

PIERRE.

Who's he disputes the judgment of the Senate?
Presumptuous rebel—on—   *Strikes* Jaffeir.

JAFFEIR.   By Heaven, you stir not.

I must be heard, I must have leave to speak.   170
Thou hast disgraced me, Pierre, by a vile blow;
Had not a dagger done thee nobler justice?
But use me as thou wilt, thou canst not wrong me,
For I am fallen beneath the basest injuries;
Yet look upon me with an eye of mercy,   175
With pity and with charity behold me;
Shut not thy heart against a friend's repentance,
But as there dwells a godlike nature in thee
Listen with mildness to my supplications.

PIERRE.

    What whining monk art thou? What holy cheat   180
    That wouldst encroach upon my credulous ears
    And cant'st thus vilely? Hence! I know thee not.
    Dissemble and be nasty. Leave me, hypocrite.

JAFFEIR.

    Not know me, Pierre?

PIERRE.   No, know thee not. What art thou?

JAFFEIR.

    Jaffeir, thy friend, thy once loved, valued friend,   185
    Though now deservedly scorned, and used most hardly.

PIERRE.

    Thou Jaffeir! Thou my once loved, valued friend!
    By Heavens, thou ly'st; the man, so called, my friend,
    Was generous, honest, faithful, just, and valiant,
    Noble in mind, and in his person lovely,   190
    Dear to my eyes and tender to my heart;
    But thou a wretched, base, false, worthless coward,
    Poor even in soul, and loathsome in thy aspect;
    All eyes must shun thee, and all hearts detest thee.
    Prithee avoid, nor longer cling thus round me,   195
    Like something baneful that my nature's chilled at.

JAFFEIR.

    I have not wronged thee, by these tears I have not.
    But still am honest, true, and hope too, valiant;
    My mind still full of thee; therefore still noble.
    Let not thy eyes then shun me, nor thy heart   200
    Detest me utterly. Oh look upon me,
    Look back and see my sad sincere submission!
    How my heart swells, as even 'twould burst my bosom;
    Fond of its jail, and laboring to be at thee!
    What shall I do? What say to make thee hear me?   205

PIERRE.

    Hast thou not wronged me? Dar'st thou call thyself
    Jaffeir, that once loved, valued friend of mine,
    And swear thou hast not wronged me? Whence these chains?
    Whence the vile death, which I may meet this moment?
    Whence this dishonor, but from thee, thou false one?   210

JAFFEIR.

    All's true, yet grant one thing, and I've done asking.

PIERRE.

What's that?

JAFFEIR.   To take thy life on such conditions
The Council have proposed. Thou and thy friends
May yet live long, and to be better treated.

PIERRE.

Life! Ask my life! Confess! Record myself   215
A villain for the privilege to breath,
And carry up and down this cursed city
A discontented and repining spirit,
Burdensome to itself a few years longer,
To lose it, may be, at last in a lewd quarrel   220
For some new friend, treacherous and false as thou art!
No, this vile world and I have long been jangling,
And cannot part on better terms than now,
When only men like thee are fit to live in't.

JAFFEIR.

By all that's just—

PIERRE.   Swear by some other powers,   225
For thou hast broke that sacred oath too lately.

JAFFEIR.

Then by that Hell I merit, I'll not leave thee,
Till to thyself, at least, thou'rt reconciled,
However thy resentments deal with me.

PIERRE.

Not leave me!

JAFFEIR.   No, thou shalt not force me from thee.   230
Use me reproachfully, and like a slave,
Tread on me, buffet me, heap wrongs on wrongs
On my poor head; I'll bear it all with patience
Shall weary out thy most unfriendly cruelty;
Lie at thy feet and kiss 'em though they spurn me,   235
Till, wounded by my sufferings, thou relent,
And raise me to thy arms with dear forgiveness.

PIERRE.

Art thou not—

JAFFEIR.   What?

PIERRE.   A traitor?

JAFFEIR.   Yes.

PIERRE.   A villain?

JAFFEIR.
   Granted.
PIERRE.   A coward, a most scandalous coward,
   Spiritless, void of honor, one who has sold   240
   Thy everlasting fame for shameless life?
JAFFEIR.
   All, all, and more, much more. My faults are numberless.
PIERRE.
   And wouldst thou have me live on terms like thine?
   Base as thou art false—
JAFFEIR.   No, 'tis to me that's granted.
   The safety of thy life was all I aimed at,   245
   In recompense for faith, and trust so broken.
PIERRE.
   I scorn it more because preserved by thee,
   And as when first my foolish heart took pity
   On thy misfortunes, sought thee in thy miseries,
   Relieved thy wants, and raised thee from thy state   250
   Of wretchedness in which thy fate had plunged thee
   To rank thee in my list of noble friends,
   All I received in surety for thy truth,
   Were unregarded oaths, and this, this dagger,
   Given with a worthless pledge, thou since hast stol'n.   255
   So I restore it back to thee again,
   Swearing by all those powers which thou hast violated,
   Never from this cursed hour to hold communion,
   Friendship or interest with thee, though our years
   Were to exceed those limited the world.   260
   Take it—farewell—for now I owe thee nothing.
JAFFEIR.
   Say thou wilt live then.
PIERRE.   For my life, dispose it
   Just as thou wilt, because 'tis what I'm tired with.
JAFFEIR.
   Oh, Pierre!
PIERRE.   No more.
JAFFEIR.   My eyes won't lose the sight of thee,
   But languish after thine, and ache with gazing.   265
PIERRE.
   Leave me—Nay, then thus, thus, I throw thee from me.
   And curses, great as is thy falsehood, catch thee.   [*Exit.*]

JAFFEIR.
Amen.
He's gone, my father, friend, preserver,
And here's the portion he has left me.   *Holds the dagger up.* 270
This dagger, well remembered, with this dagger
I gave a solemn vow of dire importance,
Parted with this and Belvidera together—
Have a care, mem'ry, drive that thought no farther.
No, I'll esteem it as a friend's last legacy,   275
Treasure it up in this wretched bosom,
Where it may grow acquainted with my heart,
That when they meet, they start not from each other.
So, now for thinking. A blow! Called traitor, villain,
Coward, dishonorable coward, fogh!   280
Oh for a long sound sleep, and so forget it!
Down, busy devil.—

Enter Belvidera.

BELVIDERA.   Whither shall I fly?
Where hide me and my miseries together?
Where's now the Roman constancy I boasted?
Sunk into trembling fears and desperation!   285
Not daring now to look up to that dear face
Which used to smile even on my faults, but down
Bending these miserable eyes to earth,
Must move in penance, and implore much mercy.
JAFFEIR.
Mercy! Kind Heaven has surely endless stores   290
Hoarded for thee of blessings yet untasted.
Let wretches loaded hard with guilt as I am,
Bow with the weight and groan beneath the burden,
Creep with a remnant of that strength th' have left,
Before the footstool of that Heaven th' have injured.   295
Oh Belvidera! I'm the wretched'st creature
E'er crawled on earth; now if thou hast virtue, help me,
Take me into thy arms, and speak the words of peace
To my divided soul that wars within me,

293. Bow with the] *Q3, W*; Bow
the *Q1-2.*

And raises every sense to my confusion.   300
By Heav'n I am tottering on the very brink
Of peace, and thou art all the hold I've left.
BELVIDERA.
    Alas! I know thy sorrows are most mighty;
    I know th' hast cause to mourn; to mourn, my Jaffeir,
    With endless cries, and never ceasing wailings;   305
    Th' hast lost—
JAFFEIR.   Oh I have lost what can't be counted.
    My friend too, Belvidera, that dear friend,
    Who, next to thee, was all my health rejoiced in,
    Has used me like a slave, shamefully used me,
    'Twould break thy pitying heart to hear the story.   310
    What shall I do? Resentment, indignation,
    Love, pity, fear, and mem'ry how I've wronged him,
    Distract my quiet with the very thought on't,
    And tear my heart to pieces in my bosom.
BELVIDERA.
    What has he done?
JAFFEIR.   Thou'dst hate me, should I tell thee.   315
BELVIDERA.
    Why?
JAFFEIR.   Oh, he has used me—yet by Heaven I bear it—
    He has used me, Belvidera—but first swear
    That when I've told thee, thou'lt not loath me utterly,
    Though vilest blots and stains appear upon me,
    But still at least with charitable goodness   320
    Be near me in the pangs of my affliction,
    Not scorn me, Belvidera, as he has done.
BELVIDERA.
    Have I then e'er been false that now I am doubted?
    Speak, what's the cause I am grown into distrust,
    Why thought unfit to hear my love's complainings?   325
JAFFEIR.
    Oh!
BELVIDERA.
    Tell me.
JAFFEIR.   Bear my failings, for they are many.
    Oh my dear angel! in that friend I've lost
    All my soul's peace; for every thought of him

Strikes my sense hard, and deads it in my brains.
Wouldst thou believe it—

BELVIDERA.   Speak.

JAFFEIR.   Before we parted,   330
Ere yet his guards had led him to his prison,
Full of severest sorrows for his suff'rings,
With eyes o'erflowing and a bleeding heart,
Humbling myself almost beneath my nature,
As at his feet I kneeled, and sued for mercy,   335
Forgetting all our friendship, all the dearness,
In which w'have lived so many years together,
With a reproachful hand, he dashed a blow,
He struck me, Belvidera, by Heaven, he struck me!
Buffeted, called me traitor, villain, coward—   340
Am I a coward? Am I a villain? Tell me:
Th'art the best judge, and mad'st me, if I am so.
Damnation. Coward!

BELVIDERA.   Oh! forgive him, Jaffeir.
And if his sufferings wound thy heart already,
What will they do tomorrow?

JAFFEIR.   Hah!

BELVIDERA.   Tomorrow,   345
When thou shalt see him stretched in all the agonies
Of a tormenting and a shameful death,
His bleeding bowels, and his broken limbs,
Insulted o'er by a vile butchering villain;
What will thy heart do then? Oh sure 'twill stream   350
Like my eyes now.

JAFFEIR.   What means thy dreadful story?
Death, and tomorrow? Broken limbs and bowels?
Insulted o'er by a vile butchering villain?
By all my fears I shall start out to madness
With barely guessing, if the truth's hid longer.   355

BELVIDERA.
The faithless Senators, 'tis they've decreed it.
They say according to our friends' request,
They shall have death, and not ignoble bondage;
Declare their promised mercy all as forfeited,
False to their oaths, and deaf to intercession;   360
Warrants are passed for public death tomorrow.

JAFFEIR.

Death! Doomed to die! Condemned unheard! Unpleaded!

BELVIDERA.

Nay, cruel'st racks and torments are preparing
To force confessions from their dying pangs.
Oh do not look so terribly upon me!   365
How your lips shake, and all your face disordered!
What means my love?

JAFFEIR.

Leave me, I charge thee leave me—strong temptations
Wake in my heart.

BELVIDERA.   For what?

JAFFEIR.   No more, but leave me.

BELVIDERA.

Why?

JAFFEIR.   Oh! by Heaven I love thee with that fondness   370
I would not have thee stay a moment longer
Near these cursed hands. Are they not cold upon thee?

BELVIDERA.

No, everlasting comfort's in thy arms,
To lean thus on thy breast is softer ease
Than downy pillows decked with leaves of roses.   375
          [*He*] *pulls the dagger half out of his bosom and puts it back again.*

JAFFEIR.

Alas, thou thinkest not of the thorns 'tis filled with;
Fly ere they gall thee. There's a lurking serpent
Ready to leap and sting thee to thy heart.
Art thou not terrified?

BELVIDERA.   No.

JAFFEIR.   Call to mind
What thou hast done, and whither thou hast brought me.   380

BELVIDERA.

Hah!

JAFFEIR.   Where's my friend? My friend, thou smiling mischief?
Nay, shrink not, now 'tis too late, thou shouldst have fled
When thy guilt first had cause, for dire revenge
Is up and raging for my friend. He groans,
Hark how he groans, his screams are in my ears   385

377. gall] *W*; call *Q1–3*.

Already; see, th' have fixed him on the wheel,
And now they tear him—Murder! Perjured Senate!
Murder—Oh!—Hark thee, traitress, thou hast done this,
Thanks to thy tears and false persuading love.

Fumbling for his dagger.

How her eyes speak! Oh thou bewitching creature!   390
Madness cannot hurt thee. Come, thou little trembler,
Creep, even into my heart, and there lie safe;
'Tis thy own citadel—Hah—Yet stand off,
Heaven must have justice, and my broken vows
Will sink me else beneath its reaching mercy;   395
I'll wink and then 'tis done—

BELVIDERA.   What means the lord
Of me, my life and love, what's in thy bosom
Thou grasp'st at so? Nay, why am I thus treated?

Draws the dagger, offers to stab her.

What wilt thou do? Ah, do not kill me, Jaffeir,
Pity these panting breasts, and trembling limbs,   400
That used to clasp thee when thy looks were milder,
That yet hang heavy on my unpurged soul,
And plunge it not into eternal darkness.

JAFFEIR.

No, Belvidera, when we parted last
I gave this dagger with thee as in trust   405
To be thy portion, if I e'er proved false.
On such condition was my truth believed;
But now 'tis forfeited and must be paid for.

Offers to stab her again.

BELVIDERA.

Oh, mercy!   *Kneeling.*

JAFFEIR.   Nay, no struggling.

BELVIDERA.   Now then kill me

Leaps upon his neck and kisses him.

While thus I cling about thy cruel neck,   410
Kiss thy revengeful lips and die in joys
Greater than any I can guess hereafter.

JAFFEIR.

I am, I am a coward; witness't, Heaven,
Witness it, earth, and every being witness!
'Tis but one blow, yet, by immortal love,   415

I cannot longer bear a thought to harm thee,
He throws away the dagger and embraces her.
The seal of Providence is sure upon thee,
And thou wert born for yet unheard of wonders:
Oh thou wert either born to save or damn me!
By all the power that's given thee o'er my soul,   420
By thy resistless tears and conquering smiles,
By the victorious love that still waits on thee:
Fly to thy cruel father; save my friend,
Or all our future quiet's lost forever.
Fall at his feet, cling round his reverend knees,   425
Speak to him with thy eyes, and with thy tears
Melt the hard heart and wake dead nature in him,
Crush him in th'arms, and torture him with thy softness.
　　　Nor, till thy prayers are granted, set him free,
　　　But conquer him, as thou hast vanquished me.   430
Exeunt ambo.

427. the] *G*; thy *Q 1–2*; his *Q 3, W.*

ACT V

[V.i]   *Enter* Priuli *solus*

PRIULI.

Why, cruel Heaven, have my unhappy days
Been lengthened to this sad one? Oh! dishonor
And deathless infamy is fall'n upon me.
Was it my fault? Am I a traitor? No.
But then, my only child, my daughter, wedded;   5
There my best blood runs foul, and a disease
Incurable has seized upon my memory
To make it rot and stink to after ages.
Cursed be the fatal minute when I got her;
Or would that I'd been anything but Man,   10
And raised an issue which would ne'er have wronged me.
The miserablest creatures (Man excepted)
Are not the less esteemed, though their posterity
Degenerate from the virtues of their fathers;
The vilest beasts are happy in their offsprings,   15
While only Man gets traitors, whores, and villains.
Cursed be the names, and some swift blow from fate
Lay his head deep, where mine may be forgotten.

            Enter Belvidera *in a long mourning veil.*

BELVIDERA.

He's there, my father, my inhuman father,
That, for three years, has left an only child   20
Exposed to all the outrages of fate,
And cruel ruin—Oh!—
PRIULI.   What child of sorrow
Art thou that com'st thus wrapped in weeds of sadness,
And mov'st as if thy steps were towards a grave?
BELVIDERA.

A wretch, who from the very top of happiness   25
Am fallen into the lowest depths of misery
And want your pitying hand to raise me up again.
PRIULI.

Indeed thou talk'st as thou hadst tasted sorrows.
Would I could help thee.

BELVIDERA.   'Tis greatly in your power.
   The world, too, speaks you charitable, and I,   30
   Who ne'er asked alms before, in that dear hope
   Am come a-begging to you, sir.
PRIULI.   For what?
BELVIDERA.
   Oh, well regard me, is this voice a strange one?
   Consider too, when beggars once pretend
   A case like mine, no little will content 'em.   35
PRIULI.
   What wouldst thou beg for?
BELVIDERA.   Pity and forgiveness.
                                        Throws up her veil.
   By the kind tender names of child and father,
   Hear my complaints and take me to your love.
PRIULI.
   My daughter?
BELVIDERA.   Yes, your daughter, by a mother
   Virtuous and noble, faithful to your honor,   40
   Obedient to your will, kind to your wishes,
   Dear to your arms; by all the joys she gave you,
   When in her blooming years she was your treasure,
   Look kindly on me; in my face behold
   The lineaments of hers y'have kissed so often,   45
   Pleading the cause of your poor cast-off child.
PRIULI.
   Thou art my daughter.
BELVIDERA.   Yes—and y'have oft told me
   With smiles of love and chaste paternal kisses,
   I'd much resemblance of my mother.
PRIULI.   Oh!
   Hadst thou inherited her matchless virtues   50
   I'd been too blessed.
BELVIDERA.   Nay, do not call to memory
   My disobedience, but let pity enter
   Into your heart, and quite deface the impression;
   For could you think how mine's perplexed, what sadness,
   Fears and despairs distract the peace within me,   55
   Oh, you would take me in your dear, dear arms,
   Hover with strong compassion o'er your young one,

4*   −79−

To shelter me with a protecting wing
From the black gathered storm, that's just, just breaking.

PRIULI.

Don't talk thus.

BELVIDERA.   Yes, I must, and you must hear too.   60
I have a husband.

PRIULI.   Damn him!

BELVIDERA.   Oh, do not curse him!
He would not speak so hard a word towards you
On any terms, howe'er he deal with me.

PRIULI.

Hah! what means my child?

BELVIDERA.   Oh, there's but this short moment
'Twixt me and fate; yet send me not with curses 65
Down to my grave, afford me one kind blessing
Before we part; just take me in your arms
And recommend me with a prayer to Heaven,
That I may die in peace, and when I'm dead—

PRIULI.

How my soul's catched!

BELVIDERA.   Lay me, I beg you, lay me 70
By the dear ashes of my tender mother.
She would have pitied me, had fate yet spared her.

PRIULI.

By Heaven, my aching heart forbodes much mischief.
Tell me thy story, for I'm still thy father.

BELVIDERA.

No, I'm contented.

PRIULI.   Speak.

BELVIDERA.   No matter.

PRIULI.   Tell me. 75
By you, blest Heaven, my heart runs o'er with fondness.

BELVIDERA.

Oh!

PRIULI. Utter't.

BELVIDERA. Oh my husband, my dear husband
Carries a dagger in his once kind bosom
To pierce the heart of your poor Belvidera.

63. howe'er] Q3, W; oh! ere Q1–2.

PRIULI.

    Kill thee?

BELVIDERA.   Yes, kill me. When he passed his faith   80
    And covenant against your state and Senate,
    He gave me up as hostage for his truth,
    With me a dagger and a dire commission,
    Whene'er he failed, to plunge it through this bosom.
    I learnt the danger, chose the hour of love   85
    T'attempt his heart, and bring it back to honor.
    Great love prevailed and blessed me with success;
    He came, confessed, betrayed his dearest friends
    For promised mercy; now they're doomed to suffer.
    Galled with remembrance of what then was sworn,   90
    If they are lost, he vows t'appease the gods
    With this poor life, and make my blood th'atonement.

PRIULI.

    Heavens!

BELVIDERA.

    Think you saw what passed at our last parting;
    Think you beheld him like a raging lion,   95
    Pacing the earth and tearing up his steps,
    Fate in his eyes, and roaring with the pain
    Of burning fury; think you saw his one hand
    Fixed on my throat, while the extended other
    Grasped a keen threat'ning dagger—oh, 'twas thus   100
    We last embraced, when, trembling with revenge,
    He dragged me to the ground, and at my bosom
    Presented horrid death, cried out, "My friends,
    Where are my friends?" Swore, wept, raged, threatened,
        loved,
    For he yet loved, and that dear love preserved me   105
    To this last trial of a father's pity.
    I fear not death, but cannot bear a thought
    That that dear hand should do th'unfriendly office.
    If I was ever then your care, now hear me:
    Fly to the Senate, save the promised lives   110
    Of his dear friends, ere mine be made the sacrifice.

PRIULI.

    Oh, my heart's comfort!

BELVIDERA.   Will you not, my father?
    Weep not, but answer me.
PRIULI.   By Heaven, I will.
    Not one of 'em but what shall be immortal.
    Canst thou forgive me all my follies past?   115
    I'll henceforth be indeed a father; never,
    Never more thus expose, but cherish thee,
    Dear as the vital warmth that feeds my life,
    Dear as these eyes that weep in fondness o'er thee.
    Peace to thy heart. Farewell.
BELVIDERA.   Go, and remember,   120
    'Tis Belvidera's life her father pleads for.   *Exeunt severally.*

[V.ii]   *Enter* Antonio.

ANTONIO.
    Hum, hum, hah, Signor Priuli, my Lord Priuli, my lord,
my lord, my lord—now, we lords love to call one another
by our titles—my lord, my lord, my lord— Pox on him, I
am a lord as well as he, and so let him fiddle. I'll warrant
him he's gone to the Senate House, and I'll be there too,   5
soon enough for somebody. Odd—here's a tickling speech
about the plot. I'll prove there's a plot with a vengeance.
Would I had it without book. Let me see—
Most Reverend Senators,
    That there is a plot, surely by this time no man that hath   10
eyes or understanding in his head will presume to doubt,
'tis as plain as the light in the cucumber—no—hold there—
cucumber does not come in yet—'tis as plain as the light in
the sun, or as the man in the moon, even at noonday. It is
indeed a pumpkin-plot, which, just as it was mellow, we   15
have gathered, and now we have gathered it, prepared and
dressed it, shall we throw it like a pickled cucumber out at
the window? No. That it is not only a bloody, horrid,
execrable, damnable, and audacious plot, but it is, as I
may so say, a saucy plot, and we all know, most reverend   20
Fathers, that what is sauce for a goose is sauce for a gander,
therefore, I say, as those bloodthirsty ganders of the conspiracy would have destroyed us geese of the Senate, let us
make haste to destroy them. So I humbly move for hang-

ing—hah, hurry durry—I think this will do, though I was   25
something out, at first, about the sun and the cucumber.

Enter Aquilina.

AQUILINA.
Good morrow, Senator.
ANTONIO.
Nacky, my dear Nacky, morrow, Nacky. Odd, I am very
brisk, very merry, very pert, very jovial—haaaaa—kiss me,
Nacky. How dost thou do, my little tory rory strumpet?   30
Kiss me, I say, hussy, kiss me.
AQUILINA.
Kiss me, Nacky! Hang you, Sir Coxcomb, hang you, sir.
ANTONIO.
Hayty tayty, is it so indeed, with all my heart, faith—
"Hey then up go we," faith—"hey then up go we," dum
dum derum dump.   *Sings.*   35
AQUILINA.
Signor.
ANTONIO.
Madonna?
AQUILINA.
Do you intend to die in your bed?
ANTONIO.
About threescore years hence much may be done, my dear.
AQUILINA.
You'll be hanged, Signor.   40
ANTONIO.
Hanged, sweetheart, prithee be quiet. Hanged quoth-a,
that's a merry conceit, with all my heart. Why, thou
jokest, Nacky, thou art given to joking, I'll swear. Well, I
protest, Nacky, nay, I must protest, and will protest that I
love joking dearly, man. And I love thee for joking, and I'll   45
kiss thee for joking, and touse thee for joking, and odd, I
have a devilish mind to take thee aside about that business
for joking too, odd I have, and "Hey then up go we," dum
dum derum dump.   *Sings.*

---

30. *tory rory*] boisterous.

AQUILINA.

    See you this, sir?   *Draws a dagger.*   50

ANTONIO.

    Oh Laud, a dagger! Oh Laud! it is naturally my aversion,
I cannot endure the sight on't. Hide it, for Heaven's sake,
I cannot look that way till it be gone—hide it, hide it, oh,
oh, hide it!

AQUILINA.

    Yes, in your heart I'll hide it.   55

ANTONIO.

    My heart, what, hide a dagger in my heart's blood!

AQUILINA.

    Yes, in thy heart, thy throat, thou pampered devil!
Thou hast helped to spoil my peace, and I'll have vengeance
On thy cursed life, for all the bloody Senate,
The perjured faithless Senate. Where's my lord,   60
My happiness, my love, my god, my hero,
Doomed by thy accursed tongue, amongst the rest,
T'a shameful rack? By all the rage that's in me
I'll be whole years in murdering thee.

ANTONIO.

    Why, Nacky, wherefore so passionate? What have I done? 65
What's the matter, my dear Nacky? Am not I thy love,
thy happiness, thy lord, thy hero, thy Senator, and everything in the world, Nacky?

AQUILINA.

    Thou! Think'st thou, thou art fit to meet my joys,
To bear the eager clasps of my embraces?   70
Give me my Pierre, or—

ANTONIO.

    Why, he's to be hanged, little Nacky, trussed up for treason,
and so forth, child.

AQUILINA.

    Thou ly'st! Stop down thy throat that hellish sentence,
Or 'tis thy last. Swear that my love shall live,   75
Or thou art dead.

ANTONIO.

    Ahhhh.

AQUILINA.   Swear to recall his doom,
    Swear at my feet, and tremble at my fury.

ANTONIO.

    I do. Now if she would but kick a little bit, one kick now.

    Ahhhh.   .   80

AQUILINA.

    Swear, or—

ANTONIO.

    I do, by these dear fragrant foots and little toes, sweet as,

    eeee, my Nacky Nacky Nacky.

AQUILINA.

    How!

ANTONIO.

    Nothing but untie thy shoestring a little, faith and troth,   85

    that's all, that's all, as I hope to live, Nacky, that's all.

AQUILINA.

    Nay, then—

ANTONIO.   Hold, hold, thy love, thy lord, thy hero,

    Shall be preserved and safe.

AQUILINA.   Or may this poniard

    Rust in thy heart.

ANTONIO.   With all my soul.

AQUILINA.   Farewell.   *Exit* Aquilina.

ANTONIO.

    Adieu. Why what a bloody-minded, inveterate, termagant   90

    strumpet have I been plagued with! Ohhh, yet more! Nay

    then I die, I die—I am dead already.

                                       Stretches himself out.

Enter Jaffeir.

JAFFEIR.

    Final destruction seize on all the world!

    Bend down, ye Heavens, and shutting round this earth,

    Crush the vile globe into its first confusion;   95

    Scorch it with elemental flames to one cursed cinder,

    And all us little creepers in't, called men,

    Burn, burn to nothing. But let Venice burn

    Hotter than all the rest; here kindle Hell

    Ne'er to extinguish, and let souls hereafter   100

    Groan here, in all those pains which mine feels now.

Enter Belvidera.

BELVIDERA.

My life— *Meeting him.*

JAFFEIR.   My plague— *Turning from her.*

BELVIDERA.   Nay then I see my ruin,

    If I must die!

JAFFEIR.   No, death's this day too busy.

    Thy father's ill-timed mercy came too late.

    I thank thee for thy labors though, and him too;   105

    But all my poor betrayed unhappy friends

    Have summons to prepare for fate's black hour;

    And yet I live.

BELVIDERA.   Then be the next my doom.

    I see thou hast passed my sentence in thy heart,

    And I'll no longer weep or plead against it,   110

    But with the humblest, most obedient patience

    Meet thy dear hands, and kiss 'em when they wound me.

    Indeed I am willing, but I beg thee do it

    With some remorse, and where thou giv'st the blow,

    View me with eyes of a relenting love,   115

    And show me pity, for 'twill sweeten justice.

JAFFEIR.

    Show pity to thee?

BELVIDERA.   Yes, and when thy hands,

    Charged with my fate, come trembling to the deed,

    As thou hast done a thousand thousand dear times

    To this poor breast, when kinder rage has brought thee,   120

    When our stinged hearts have leaped to meet each other,

    And melting kisses sealed our lips together,

    When joys have left me gasping in thy arms,

    So let my death come now, and I'll not shrink from't.

JAFFEIR.

    Nay, Belvidera, do not fear my cruelty,   125

    Nor let the thoughts of death perplex thy fancy,

    But answer me to what I shall demand,

    With a firm temper and unshaken spirit.

BELVIDERA.

    I will when I've done weeping—

JAFFEIR.   Fie, no more on't—

    How long is't since the miserable day   130

    We wedded first—

BELVIDERA.   Ohhh.

JAFFEIR.   Nay, keep in thy tears,
   Lest they unman me too.

BELVIDERA.   Heaven knows I cannot:
   The words you utter sound so very sadly
   These streams will follow.

JAFFEIR.   Come, I'll kiss 'em dry then.

BELVIDERA.
   But, was't a miserable day?

JAFFEIR.   A cursed one.   135

BELVIDERA.
   I thought it otherwise, and you've oft sworn
   In the transporting hours of warmest love
   When sure you spoke the truth, you've sworn you blessed it.

JAFFEIR.
   'Twas a rash oath.

BELVIDERA.   Then why am I not cursed too?

JAFFEIR.
   No, Belvidera; by th'eternal truth,   140
   I dote with too much fondness.

BELVIDERA.   Still so kind?
   Still then do you love me?

JAFFEIR.   Nature, in her workings,
   Inclines not with more ardor to Creation,
   Than I do now towards thee; man ne'er was blessed,
   Since the first pair first met, as I have been.   145

BELVIDERA.
   Then sure you will not curse me.

JAFFEIR.   No, I'll bless thee.
   I came on purpose, Belvidera, to bless thee.
   'Tis now, I think, three years w' have lived together.

BELVIDERA.
   And may no fatal minute ever part us,
   Till, reverend grown, for age and love, we go   150
   Down to one grave, as our last bed, together,
   There sleep in peace till an eternal morning.

JAFFEIR.
   When will that be?   *Sighing.*

BELVIDERA.   I hope long ages hence.

JAFFEIR.
   Have I not hitherto (I beg thee tell me

Thy very fears) used thee with tender'st love?   155
Did e'er my soul rise up in wrath against thee?
Did I e'er frown when Belvidera smiled,
Or, by the least unfriendly word, betray
A bating passion? Have I ever wronged thee?

BELVIDERA.
No.

JAFFEIR.
Has my heart, or have my eyes e'er wandered   160
To any other woman?

BELVIDERA.   Never, never—
I were the worst of false ones should I accuse thee.
I own I've been too happy, blessed above
My sex's charter.

JAFFEIR.   Did I not say I came
To bless thee?

BELVIDERA.   Yes.

JAFFEIR.   Then hear me, bounteous Heaven;   165
Pour down your blessing on this beauteous head,
Where everlasting sweets are always springing.
With a continual giving hand, let peace,
Honor and safety always hover round her;
Feed her with plenty, let her eyes ne'er see   170
A sight of sorrow, nor her heart know mourning;
Crown all her days with joy, her nights with rest,
Harmless as her own thoughts, and prop her virtue
To bear the loss of one that too much loved,
And comfort her with patience in our parting.   175

BELVIDERA.
How, parting, parting!

JAFFEIR.   Yes, forever parting.
I have sworn, Belvidera. By yon Heaven,
That best can tell how much I lose to leave thee,
We part this hour forever.

BELVIDERA.   Oh, call back
Your cruel blessings, stay with me and curse me!   180

JAFFEIR.
No, 'tis resolved.

BELVIDERA.   Then hear me too, just Heaven,
Pour down your curses on this wretched head

-88-

With never-ceasing vengeance; let despair,
Danger or infamy, nay all surround me;   185
Starve me with wantings, let my eyes ne'er see
A sight of comfort, nor my heart know peace,
But dash my days with sorrow, nights with horrors
Wild as my own thoughts now, and let loose fury
To make me mad enough for what I lose,
If I must lose him. If I must! I will not.   190
Oh turn and hear me!
JAFFEIR.   Now hold, heart, or never.
BELVIDERA.
By all the tender days we have lived together,
By all our charming nights, and joys that crowned 'em,
Pity my sad condition. Speak, but speak.
JAFFEIR.
Ohhh.
BELVIDERA.
          By these arms that now cling round thy neck,   195
By this dear kiss and by ten thousand more,
By these poor streaming eyes—
JAFFEIR.   Murder! Unhold me!
By th'immortal destiny that doomed me   *Draws his dagger.*
To this cursed minute, I'll not live one longer.
Resolve to let me go or see me fall—   200
BELVIDERA.
Hold, sir, be patient.   *Passing bell tolls.*
JAFFEIR.   Hark, the dismal bell
Tolls out for death. I must attend its call too,
For my poor friend, my dying Pierre expects me.
He sent a message to require I'd see him
Before he died, and take his last forgiveness.   205
Farewell forever.
BELVIDERA.   Leave thy dagger with me.
Bequeath me something—not one kiss at parting?
Oh my poor heart, when wilt thou break?
                    Going out [he] looks back at her.
JAFFEIR.   Yet stay.
We have a child, as yet a tender infant,
Be a kind mother to him when I am gone,   210
Breed him in virtue and the paths of honor,

But let him never know his father's story;
I charge thee guard him from the wrongs my fate
May do his future fortune or his name.
Now—nearer yet—   *Approaching each other.* 215
Oh that my arms were riveted
Thus round thee ever! But my friends, my oath!
This and no more.   *Kisses her.*
BELVIDERA.   Another, sure another,
    For that poor little one you've ta'en care of,
    I'll giv't him truly.
JAFFEIR.   So, now farewell.
BELVIDERA.   Forever?   220
JAFFEIR.
    Heaven knows forever. All good angels guard thee.   [*Exit.*]
BELVIDERA.
    All ill ones sure had charge of me this moment.
    Cursed be my days, and doubly cursed my nights,
    Which I must now mourn out in widowed tears;
    Blasted be every herb and fruit and tree,   225
    Cursed be the rain that falls upon the earth,
    And may the general curse reach man and beast.
    Oh give me daggers, fire, or water;
    How I could bleed, how burn, how drown, the waves
    Huzzing and booming round my sinking head,   230
    Till I descended to the peaceful bottom!
    Oh there's all quiet, here all rage and fury.
    The air's too thin, and pierces my weak brain,
    I long for thick substantial sleep. Hell, Hell,
    Burst from the center, rage and roar aloud,   235
    If thou art half so hot, so mad as I am.

                    Enter Priuli *and* Servants.

    Who's there?
PRIULI.   Run, seize and bring her safely home,
                                        They seize her.
    Guard her as you would life. Alas poor creature!
BELVIDERA.
    What? To my husband then conduct me quickly.
    Are all things ready? Shall we die most gloriously?   240
    Say not a word of this to my old father,

Murmuring streams, soft shades, and springing flowers,
Lutes, laurels, seas of milk, and ships of amber.   *Exeunt.*

[V.iii]
Scene opening discovers a scaffold and a wheel prepared for the executing of
Pierre; *then enter* Officers, Pierre, *and Guards, a* Friar, Executioner, *and*
a great Rabble.

OFFICER.
    Room room there—stand all by, make room for the prisoner.
PIERRE.
    My friend not come yet?
FATHER.   Why are you so obstinate?
PIERRE.
    Why you so troublesome, that a poor wretch
    Cannot die in peace,
    But you, like ravens, will be croaking round him?   5
FATHER.
    Yet, Heaven—
PIERRE.   I tell thee Heaven and I are friends.
    I ne'er broke peace with't yet by cruel murders,
    Rapine, or perjury, or vile deceiving,
    But lived in moral justice towards all men,
    Nor am a foe to the most strong believers   10
    Howe'er my own short-sighted faith confine me.
FATHER.
    But an all-seeing Judge—
PIERRE.   You say my conscience
    Must be mine accuser. I have searched that conscience,
    And find no records there of crimes that scare me.
FATHER.
    'Tis strange you should want faith.
PIERRE.   You want to lead   15
    My reason blindfold, like a hampered lion,
    Checked of its nobler vigor; then, when baited
    Down to obedient tameness, make it couch,
    And show strange tricks which you call signs of faith.
    So silly souls are gulled and you get money.   20
    Away, no more. Captain, I would hereafter
    This fellow write no lies of my conversion,

Because he has crept upon my troubled hours.

Enter Jaffeir.

JAFFEIR.

    Hold. Eyes, be dry; heart, strengthen me to bear
    This hideous sight, and humble me to take   25
    The last forgiveness of a dying friend,
    Betrayed by my vile falsehood to his ruin.
    Oh Pierre!

PIERRE.   Yet nearer.

JAFFEIR.   Crawling on my knees,
    And prostrate on the earth, let me approach thee.
    How shall I look up to thy injured face,   30
    That always used to smile with friendship on me?
    It darts an air of so much manly virtue,
    That I, methinks, look little in thy sight,
    And stripes are fitter for me than embraces.

PIERRE.

    Dear to my arms, though thou hast undone my fame,   35
    I cannot forget to love thee. Prithee, Jaffeir,
    Forgive that filthy blow my passion dealt thee;
    I am now preparing for the land of peace,
    And fain would have the charitable wishes
    Of all good men, like thee, to bless my journey.   40

JAFFEIR.

    Good! I am the vilest creature, worse than e'er
    Suffered the shameful fate thou art going to taste of.
    Why was I sent for to be used thus kindly?
    Call, call me villain, as I am, describe
    The foul complexion of my hateful deeds,   45
    Lead me to the rack, and stretch me in thy stead,
    I've crimes enough to give it its full load,
    And do it credit. Thou wilt but spoil the use on't,
    And honest men hereafter bear its figure
    About 'em, as a charm from treacherous friendship.   50

OFFICER.

    The time grows short, your friends are dead already.

25. me to take] *G*; me, take *Q1–2*;
me: Take *Q3*, *W*.

JAFFEIR.

Dead!

PIERRE.

Yes, dead, Jaffeir. They've all died like men too,
Worthy their character.

JAFFEIR.   And what must I do?

PIERRE.

Oh, Jaffeir!

JAFFEIR.   Speak aloud thy burdened soul,   55
And tell thy troubles to thy tortured friend.

PIERRE.

Friend! Couldst thou yet be a friend, a generous friend,
I might hope comfort from thy noble sorrows.
Heaven knows I want a friend.

JAFFEIR.   And I a kind one,
That would not thus scorn my repenting virtue,   60
Or think when he is to die, my thoughts are idle.

PIERRE.

No! Live, I charge thee, Jaffeir.

JAFFEIR.   Yes, I will live,
But it shall be to see thy fall revenged
At such a rate, as Venice long shall groan for.

PIERRE.

Wilt thou?

JAFFEIR.   I will, by Heaven.

PIERRE.   Then still thou'rt noble,   65
And I forgive thee, oh—yet—shall I trust thee?

JAFFEIR.

No. I've been false already.

PIERRE.   Dost thou love me?

JAFFEIR.

Rip up my heart, and satisfy thy doubtings.

PIERRE.

Curse on this weakness.   *He weeps.*

JAFFEIR.   Tears! Amazement! Tears!
I never saw thee melted thus before;   70
And know there's something lab'ring in thy bosom
That must have vent. Though I'm a villain, tell me.

PIERRE.

Seest thou that engine?   *Pointing to the wheel.*

JAFFEIR.

    Why?

PIERRE.

    Is't fit a soldier, who has lived with honor,   75
    Fought nations' quarrels, and been crowned with conquest,
    Be exposed a common carcass on a wheel?

JAFFEIR.

    Hah!

PIERRE.   Speak! Is't fitting?

JAFFEIR.   Fitting?

PIERRE.   Yes, is't fitting?

JAFFEIR.

    What's to be done?

PIERRE.   I'd have thee undertake
    Something that's noble, to preserve my memory   80
    From the disgrace that's ready to attaint it.

OFFICER.

    The day grows late, sir.

PIERRE.   I'll make haste! Oh Jaffeir,
    Though thou'st betrayed me, do me some way justice.

JAFFEIR.

    No more of that. Thy wishes shall be satisfied.
    I have a wife and she shall bleed, my child too   85
    Yield up his little throat, and all t'appease thee—

                            Going away. Pierre *holds him.*

PIERRE.

    No—this—no more!   *He whispers* Jaffeir.

JAFFEIR.   Hah! is't then so?

PIERRE.   Most certainly.

JAFFEIR.

    I'll do't.

PIERRE.   Remember.

OFFICER.   Sir.

PIERRE.   Come, now I'm ready.

         He and Jaffeir *ascend the scaffold.*

    Captain, you should be a gentleman of honor,
    Keep off the rabble, that I may have room   90
    To entertain my fate, and die with decency.
    Come!

      Takes off his gown. Executioner *prepares to bind him.*

FATHER.
Son!

PIERRE. Hence, tempter.

OFFICER.   Stand off, priest.

PIERRE.   I thank you, sir.
(*To* Jaffeir.) You'll think on't?

JAFFEIR.   'Twon't grow stale before tomorrow.

PIERRE.
Now, Jaffeir! now I am going. Now—
                            Executioner *having bound him.*

JAFFEIR.   Have at thee,   95
Thou honest heart, then—here—   *Stabs him.*
And this is well too.   *Then stabs himself.*

FATHER.
Damnable deed!

PIERRE.   Now thou hast indeed been faithful.
This was done nobly—we have deceived the Senate.

JAFFEIR.
Bravely.

PIERRE.   Ha ha ha—oh oh—   *Dies.*

JAFFEIR.   Now, ye cursed rulers,   100
Thus of the blood y'have shed I make libation,
And sprinkled mingling: may it rest upon you,
And all your race. Be henceforth peace a stranger
Within your walls; let plagues and famine waste
Your generations—oh poor Belvidera!   105
Sir, I have a wife, bear this in safety to her,
                            [*Gives* Officer *the dagger.*]
A token that with my dying breath I blessed her,
And the dear little infant left behind me.
I am sick—I'm quiet—   Jaffeir *dies.*

OFFICER.   Bear this news to the Senate,
And guard their bodies till there's farther order.   110
Heav'n grant I die so well—   *Scene shuts upon them.*

[V.iv]
Soft music. Enter Belvidera *distracted, led by two of her* Women, Priuli *and*
Servants.

PRIULI.
Strengthen her heart with patience, pitying Heav'n.

BELVIDERA.
    Come come come come come. Nay, come to bed!
    Prithee my love. The winds! hark how they whistle!
    And the rain beats. Oh how the weather shrinks me!
    You are angry now, who cares? Pish, no indeed.   5
    Choose then, I say you shall not go, you shall not.
    Whip your ill nature, get you gone then! Oh,
                         Jaffeir's ghost rises.
    Are you returned? See, father, here he's come again.
    Am I to blame to love him! Oh thou dear one.   *Ghost sinks.*
    Why do you fly me? Are you angry still then?   10
    Jaffeir! where art thou? Father, why do you do thus?
    Stand off, don't hide him from me. He's here somewhere.
    Stand off I say! What, gone? Remember't, tyrant!
    I may revenge myself for this trick one day.

              Enter Officer *and others.*

    I'll do't—I'll do't. Renault's a nasty fellow.   15
    Hang him, hang him, hang him.
PRIULI.   News, what news?
OFFICER (*whispers* Priuli).   Most sad, sir.
    Jaffeir upon the scaffold, to prevent
    A shameful death, stabbed Pierre, and next himself.
    Both fell together.
PRIULI.   Daughter.

    The Ghosts of Jaffeir *and* Pierre *rise together both bloody.*

BELVIDERA.   Hah, look there!
    My husband bloody, and his friend too! Murder!   20
    Who has done this? Speak to me, thou sad vision,   *Ghosts sink.*
    On these poor trembling knees I beg it. —Vanished—
    Here they went down. Oh I'll dig, dig the den up.
    You shan't delude me thus. Hoa, Jaffeir, Jaffeir!
    Peep up and give me but a look. I have him!   25
    I've got him, father! Oh now how I'll smuggle him!
    My love! my dear! my blessing! Help me, help me!
    They have hold on me, and drag me to the bottom.
    Nay—now they pull so hard—farewell—   *She dies.*

---

26. *smuggle*] cuddle.

MAID.   She's dead.

    Breathless and dead.

PRIULI.   Then guard me from the sight on't.   30
    Lead me into some place that's fit for mourning,
    Where the free air, light, and the cheerful sun
    May never enter. Hang it round with black;
    Set up one taper that may last a day,
    As long as I've to live, and there all leave me;   35
        Sparing no tears when you this tale relate,
        But bid all cruel fathers dread my fate.

Curtain falls. Exeunt omnes.

FINIS

EPILOGUE

The text is done, and now for application,
And when that's ended pass your approbation.
Though the conspiracy's prevented here,
Methinks I see another hatching there;
And there's a certain faction fain would sway,   5
If they had strength enough and damn this play;
But this the author bade me boldly say:
If any take his plainness in ill part,
He's glad on't from the bottom of his heart.
Poets in honor of the truth should write   10
With the same spirit brave men for it fight;
And though against him causeless hatreds rise,
And daily where he goes of late, he spies
The scowls of sullen and revengeful eyes;
'Tis what he knows with much contempt to bear,   15
And serves a cause too good to let him fear.
He fears no poison from an incensed drab,
No ruffian's five-foot sword, nor rascal's stab;
Nor any other snares of mischief laid,
Not a Rose-alley cudgel-ambuscade   20
From any private cause where malice reigns,
Or general pique all blockheads have to brains.
Nothing shall daunt his pen when truth does call,
No, not the picture-mangler at Guildhall.
The rebel tribe, of which that vermin's one,   25
Have now set forward and their course begun;

2. ended] *F2, Q1–3, W*; done *F1*.
2. pass] *Q1–3, W*; pray give *F1*; give *F2*.
7. bade me boldly] *F1, Q1–3, W*; boldly bade me *F2*.
11. spirit] *Q1–3, W*; courage *F1–2*.
14. scowls] *F1, Q1–3, W*; frowns *F2*.
22.] A general sign all blockheads have no brains *F1*; Or general pique that blockheads have to brains *F2*.
23.] Nothing doth damn his pen when truth doth call *F1*; Nothing shall daunt his pen when truth doth call *F2*.
24. at] *F2, Q1–3, W*; of *F1*.
26. their] *F1, Q1–3, W*; the *F2*.

20. *Rose-alley*] alluding to the assault on Dryden made there December 18, 1679, presumably as a warning to him about his satires.
24. *picture-mangler*] "The rascal that cut the Duke of York's picture" (Otway's note). The incident occurred in January, 1682.

And while that prince's figure they deface,
As they before had massacred his name,
Durst their base fears but look him in the face,
They'd use his person as they've used his fame;   30
A face, in which such lineaments they read
Of that great martyr's, whose rich blood they shed,
That their rebellious hate they still retain,
And in his son would murder him again.
With indignation then, let each brave heart   35
Rouse and unite to take his injured part;
Till royal love and goodness call him home,
And songs of triumph meet him as he come;
Till Heaven his honor and our peace restore,
And villains never wrong his virtue more.   40

---

27. while] *F2, Q1–3, W*; whil'st *F1*.
28. name] *F2, Q1–3, W*; fame *F1*. *In F2 ll. 28 and 29 are transposed.*
31. read] *F2, Q1–3, W*; dread *F1*.

32. martyr's] *F1, Q1–3, W*; martyr *F2*.
33. retain] *F1, Q1–3, W*; maintain *F2*.
39. our] *F1, Q1–3, W*; his *F2*.

32. *martyr's*] Charles I.

Appendix A

Prologues and Epilogues for the Duke and Duchess of York

A special prologue by Dryden and an epilogue by Otway were written for the visit of the Duke of York to the theater, April 21, 1682, and again for the visit of the Duchess on May 31.

Prologue for April 21, 1682:

In those cold regions which no summers cheer,
Where brooding darkness covers half the year,
To hollow caves the shivering natives go,
Bears range abroad, and hunt in tracks of snow;
But when the tedious twilight wears away,   5
And stars grow paler at th'approach of day,
The longing crowds to frozen mountains run,
Happy who first can see the glimmering sun!
The surly savage offspring disappear,
And curse the bright successor of the year.   10
Yet, though rough bears in covert seek defense,⎫
White foxes stay, with seeming innocence: ⎬
That crafty kind with daylight can dispense. ⎭
Still we are thronged so full with Reynard's race,
That loyal subjects scarce can find a place;   15
Thus modest Truth is cast behind the crowd:
Truth speaks too low, Hypocrisy too loud.
Let 'em be first to flatter in success,
Duty can stay, but Guilt has need to press.
Once, when true zeal the sons of God did call   20
To make their solemn show at Heaven's Whitehall,
The fawning Devil appeared among the rest,
And made as good a courtier as the best.
The friends of Job, who railed at him before,

Came cap in hand when he had three times more.   25
Yet late repentance may, perhaps, be true;
Kings can forgive if rebels can but sue:
A tyrant's pow'r in rigor is expressed,
The father yearns in the true prince's breast.
We grant an o'ergrown Whig no grace can mend;   30
But most are babes that know not they offend.
The crowd, to restless motion still inclined,
Are clouds that rack according to the wind.
Driv'n by their chiefs they storms of hailstones pour;
Then mourn, and soften to a silent shower.   35
O welcome to this much offending land
The prince that brings forgiveness in his hand!
Thus angels on glad messages appear;
Their first salute commands us not to fear.
Thus Heav'n, that could constrain us to obey⎫   40
(With rev'rence if we might presume to say),⎬
Seems to relax the rights of sov'reign sway,⎭
Permits to Man the choice of good and ill,
And makes us happy by our own free-will.

Epilogue for April 21:

When too much plenty, luxury, and ease,
Had surfeited this isle to a disease;
When noisome blains did its best parts o'erspread,
And on the rest their dire infection shed;
Our great physician, who the nature knew⎫   5
Of the distemper, and from whence it grew,⎬
Fixed for three kingdoms' quiet (sir) on you.⎭
He cast his searching eyes o'er all the frame,
And finding whence before one sickness came,
How once before our mischiefs fostered were,   10
Knew well your virtue, and applied you there;
Where so your goodness, so your justice swayed,
You but appeared, and the wild plague was stayed.
When, from the filthy dunghill-faction bred,⎫
New-formed rebellion durst rear up its head,⎬   15
Answer me all: who struck the monster dead?⎭

---

11. *applied you there*] The Duke had been sent to Scotland.

See, see, the injured prince, and bless his name,
Think on the martyr from whose loins he came,
Think on the blood was shed for you before,
And curse the parricides that thirst for more. 20
His foes are yours, then of their wiles beware,
Lay, lay him in your hearts, and guard him there;
Where let his wrongs your zeal for him improve,
He wears a sword will justify your love,
With blood still ready for your good t'expend, 25
And has a heart that ne'er forgot his friend.
His duteous loyalty before you lay,
And learn of him, unmurm'ring to obey.
Think what he'as borne, your quiet to restore,
Repent your madness and rebel no more. 30
No more let bout-feus hope to lead petitions,
Scriv'ners to be treas'rers; pedlars, politicians;
Nor every fool, whose wife has tripped at Court,
Pluck up a spirit, and turn rebel for't.
In lands where cuckolds multiply like ours, 35
What prince can be too jealous of their powers,
Or can too often think himself alarmed?
They're malcontents that ev'rywhere go armed;
And when the horned herd's together got,
Nothing portends a commonwealth like that. 40
Cast, cast your idols off, your gods of wood,
Ere yet Philistines fatten with your blood;
Renounce your priests of Baal with amen-faces,
Your Wapping feasts, and your Mile-End high places.
Nail all your medals on the gallows post, 45
In recompense th'original was lost.
At these, illustrious repentance pay,
In his kind hands your humble off'rings lay;
Let royal pardon be by him implored,
Th'attoning brother of your angered lord. 50

---

31. *bout-feus*] incendiaries.
31. *petitions*] for the recall of Parliament.
32. *Scriv'ners*] clerks.
44. *Wapping . . . Mile-End*] The Whigs' strength was in the East End.
45. *medals*] alluding to the medal struck to celebrate the failure of the indictment of Shaftesbury for high treason, November 24, 1681.

He only brings a medicine fit to assuage
A people's folly, and roused monarch's rage;
An infant prince yet lab'ring in the womb,⎤
Fated with wond'rous happiness to come, ⎬
He goes to fetch the mighty blessing home.⎦   55
Send all your wishes with him, let the air ⎤
With gentle breezes waft it safely here, ⎬
The seas, like what they'll carry, calm and fair;⎦
Let the illustrious mother touch our land
Mildly, as hereafter may her son command;   60
While our glad monarch welcomes her to shore,
With kind assurance she shall part no more.
Be the majestic babe then smiling born,
And all good signs of fate his birth adorn,
So live and grow, a constant pledge to stand   65
Of Caesar's love to an obedient land.

Prologue for May 31, 1682:

When factious rage to cruel exile drove
The Queen of Beauty, and the Court of Love,
The Muses drooped, with their forsaken Arts,
And the sad Cupids broke their useless darts.
Our fruitful plains to wilds and deserts turned,   5
Like Eden's face when banished Man it mourned;
Love was no more when Loyalty was gone,
The great supporter of his awful throne.
Love could no longer after beauty stay, ⎤
But wandered northward to the verge of day, ⎬   10
As if the sun and he had lost their way. ⎦
But now th'illustrious nymph returned again,
Brings every Grace triumphant in her train;
The wond'ring Nereids, though they raised a storm,
Foreslowed her passage to behold her form;   15
Some cried a Venus, some a Thetis passed:
But this was not so fair, nor that so chaste.
Far from her sight flew Faction, Strife, and Pride;

53. *infant prince*] The Duchess's child, however, proved to be a daughter.
55. *fetch . . . home*] The Duchess was in Scotland.

And Envy did but look on her, and died.
Whate'er we suffered from our sullen fate,   20
Her sight is purchased at an easy rate;
Three gloomy years against this day were set:
But this one mighty sum has cleared the debt;
Like Joseph's dream, but with a better doom,
The famine passed, the plenty still to come.   25
For her the weeping heav'ns become serene,
For her the ground is clad in cheerful green;
For her the nightingales are taught to sing,
And Nature has for her delayed the spring.
The Muse resumes her long-forgotten lays,   30
And Love, restored, his ancient realm surveys,
Recalls our beauties, and revives our plays;
His waste dominions peoples once again,
And from her presence dates his second reign.
But awful charms on her fair forehead sit,   35
Dispensing what she never will admit;
Pleasing yet cold, like Cynthia's silver beam,
The people's wonder, and the poet's theme.
Distempered Zeal, Sedition, cankered Hate,
No more shall vex the Church, and tear the State;   40
No more shall Faction civil discords move,
Or only discords of too tender love:
Discord like that of music's various parts,
Discord that makes the harmony of hearts,
Discord that only this dispute shall bring: 45
Who best shall love the Duke, and serve the King.

Epilogue for May 31:

All you, who this day's jubilee attend,
And every loyal Muse's loyal friend
That comes to treat your longing wishes here,
Turn your desiring eyes and feast 'em, there.
Thus falling on your knees with me implore,   5
May this poor land ne'er lose that presence more.
But if there any in this circle be,
That come so cursed to envy what they see
(From the dull fool that would be great too soon,

To the dull knave that writ the last lampoon!)   10
Let such, as victims to that beauty's fame,
Hang their vile blasted heads and die with shame.
Our mighty blessing is at last returned,
The joy arrived for which so long we mourned;
From whom our present peace we expect increased,   15
And all our future generations blessed.
Time have a care: bring safe the hour of joy
When some blessed tongue proclaims a royal boy;
And when 'tis born, let Nature's hand be strong,
Bless him with days of strength and make 'em long,   20
Till charged with honors we behold him stand, ⎤
Three kingdoms' banners waiting his command, ⎬
His father's conquering sword within his hand: ⎦
Then th'English lions in the air advance, ⎤
And with them roaring music to the dance, ⎬   25
Carry a *Quo Warranto* into France. ⎦

26. *Quo Warranto*] ask the king of France what warrant he had to govern the kingdom: an allusion to Charles II's maneuvers against the independence of the City of London in which he demanded the grounds of their municipal privileges.

Appendix B

Chronology

Approximate dates are indicated by *. Dates for plays are those on which they were first made public, either on stage or in print.

Political and Literary Events	*Life and Works of Thomas Otway*
1631 Death of Donne. John Dryden born.	
1633 Samuel Pepys born.	
1635 Sir George Etherege born.*	
1640 Aphra Behn born.*	
1641 William Wycherley born.*	
1642 First Civil War began (ended 1646). Theaters closed by Parliament. Thomas Shadwell born.*	
1648 Second Civil War. Nathaniel Lee born.*	
1649 Execution of Charles I.	
1650 Jeremy Collier born.	
1651. Hobbes' *Leviathan* published.	
1652 First Dutch War began (ended 1654).	March 3, Thomas Otway born; the son of Humphrey Otway, Rector of Woolbeding, Sussex.

1656
D'Avenant's *THE SIEGE OF RHODES* performed at Rutland House.

1657
John Dennis born.

1658
Death of Oliver Cromwell.
D'Avenant's *THE CRUELTY OF THE SPANIARDS IN PERU* performed at the Cockpit.

1660
Restoration of Charles II.
Theatrical patents granted to Thomas Killigrew and Sir William D'Avenant, authorizing them to form, respectively, the King's and the Duke of York's Companies.
Pepys began his diary.

1661
Cowley's *THE CUTTER OF COLEMAN STREET*.
D'Avenant's *THE SIEGE OF RHODES* (expanded to two parts).

1662
Charter granted to the Royal Society.

1663
Dryden's *THE WILD GALLANT*.
Tuke's *THE ADVENTURES OF FIVE HOURS*.

1664
Sir John Vanbrugh born.
Dryden's *THE RIVAL LADIES*.
Dryden and Howard's *THE INDIAN QUEEN*.
Etherege's *THE COMICAL REVENGE*.

1665
Second Dutch War began (ended 1667).
Great Plague.

Dryden's *THE INDIAN EM-PEROR.*
Orrery's *MUSTAPHA.*

1666
Fire of London.
Death of James Shirley.

1667
Jonathan Swift born.
Milton's *Paradise Lost* published.
Sprat's *The History of the Royal Society* published.
Dryden's *SECRET LOVE.*

1668
Death of D'Avenant.
Dryden made Poet Laureate.
Dryden's *An Essay of Dramatic Poesy* published.
Shadwell's *THE SULLEN LOVERS.*

Admitted as a Commoner of Winchester College.

1669
Pepys terminated his diary.
Susannah Centlivre born.

Admitted as a Commoner of Christ Church, Oxford (May).

1670
William Congreve born.
Dryden's *THE CONQUEST OF GRANADA,* Part I.

1671
Dorset Garden Theatre (Duke's Company) opened.
Colley Cibber born.
Milton's *Paradise Regained* and *Samson Agonistes* published.
Dryden's *THE CONQUEST OF GRANADA,* Part II.
THE REHEARSAL, by the Duke of Buckingham and others.
Wycherley's *LOVE IN A WOOD.*

His father died (February).
Left Oxford without taking a degree and sought a living in the London theatrical world.

1672
Third Dutch War began (ended 1674).

Joseph Addison born.
Richard Steele born.
Dryden's *MARRIAGE A LA MODE.*

1674
New Drury Lane Theatre (King's Company) opened.
Death of Milton.
Nicholas Rowe born.
Thomas Rymer's *Reflections on Aristotle's Treatise of Poesy* (translation of Rapin) published.

1675
Dryden's *AURENG-ZEBE.*
Wycherley's *THE COUNTRY WIFE.**

ALCIBIADES produced by the Duke's Company at Dorset Garden in September.

1676
Etherege's *THE MAN OF MODE.*
Shadwell's *THE VIRTUOSO.*
Wycherley's *THE PLAIN DEALER.*

DON CARLOS produced at Dorset Garden in June, and *TITUS AND BERENICE* and *THE CHEATS OF SCAPIN* about December.

1677
Aphra Behn's *THE ROVER.*
Dryden's *ALL FOR LOVE.*
Lee's *THE RIVAL QUEENS.*
Rymer's *Tragedies of the Last Age Considered* published.

Attacked by Rochester in *A Session of the Poets.* (Otway believed Elkanah Settle to be the author.)

1678
Popish Plot.
George Farquhar born.
Bunyan's *Pilgrim's Progress* (Part I) published.

Military service in Flanders. Commissioned first as an ensign (February), then as a lieutenant (November).
FRIENDSHIP IN FASHION produced at Dorset Garden in April.

1679
Exclusion Bill introduced.
Death of Thomas Hobbes.
Death of Roger Boyle, Earl of Orrery.
Charles Johnson born.

Disbandment from the army (June).
THE HISTORY AND FALL OF CAIUS MARIUS produced at Dorset Garden in August or September.

1680

Death of Samuel Butler.
Death of John Wilmot, Earl of Rochester.
Dryden's *THE SPANISH FRIAR*.
Lee's *LUCIUS JUNIUS BRUTUS*.

THE ORPHAN (February or March) and *THE SOLDIER'S FORTUNE* (March) both produced at Dorset Garden.
The Poet's Complaint of his Muse published (February).
Awarded the degree of M.A. at Cambridge (September).

1681

Charles II dissolved Parliament at Oxford.
Dryden's *Absalom and Achitophel* published.
Tate's adaptation of *KING LEAR*.

1682

The King's and the Duke of York's Companies merged into the United Company.
Dryden's *The Medal, MacFlecknoe*, and *Religio Laici* published.

VENICE PRESERVED produced at Dorset Garden in February.

1683

Rye House Plot.
Death of Thomas Killigrew.
Crowne's *CITY POLITIQUES*.

THE ATHEIST produced at Dorset Garden (between June and November).

1685

Death of Charles II; accession of James II.
Revocation of the Edict of Nantes.
The Duke of Monmouth's Rebellion.
John Gay born.
Crowne's *SIR COURTLY NICE*.
Dryden's *ALBION AND ALBANIUS*.

Died April 14 in indigence on Tower Hill.

1687

Death of the Duke of Buckingham.
Dryden's *The Hind and the Panther* published.
Newton's *Principia* published.

1688

The Revolution.
Alexander Pope born.

Shadwell's *THE SQUIRE OF ALSATIA.*

1689

The War of the League of Augsburg began (ended 1697).

Toleration Act.

Death of Aphra Behn.

Shadwell made Poet Laureate.

Dryden's *DON SEBASTIAN.*

Shadwell's *BURY FAIR.*

1690

Battle of the Boyne.

Locke's *Two Treatises of Government* and *An Essay Concerning Human Understanding* published.

1691

Death of Etherege.*

Langbaine's *An Account of the English Dramatic Poets* published.

1692

Death of Lee.

Death of Shadwell.

Tate made Poet Laureate.

1693

George Lillo born.*

Rymer's *A Short View of Tragedy* published.

Congreve's *THE OLD BACHELOR.*

1694

Death of Queen Mary.

Southerne's *THE FATAL MARRIAGE.*

1695

Group of actors led by Thomas Betterton left Drury Lane and established a new company at Lincoln's Inn Fields.

Congreve's *LOVE FOR LOVE.*

Southerne's *OROONOKO.*

1696

Cibber's *LOVE'S LAST SHIFT.*

Vanbrugh's *THE RELAPSE.*

1697

Treaty of Ryswick ended the War of the League of Augsburg.

Charles Macklin born.

Congreve's *THE MOURNING BRIDE*.

Vanbrugh's *THE PROVOKED WIFE*.

1698

Collier controversy started with the publication of *A Short View of the Immorality and Profaneness of the English Stage*.

1699

Farquhar's *THE CONSTANT COUPLE*.

1700

Death of Dryden.

Blackmore's *Satire against Wit* published.

Congreve's *THE WAY OF THE WORLD*.

1701

Act of Settlement.

War of the Spanish Succession began (ended 1713).

Death of James II.

Rowe's *TAMERLANE*.

Steele's *THE FUNERAL*.

1702

Death of William III; accession of Anne.

The Daily Courant began publication.

Cibber's *SHE WOULD AND SHE WOULD NOT*.

1703

Death of Samuel Pepys.

Rowe's *THE FAIR PENITENT*.

1704

Capture of Gibraltar; Battle of Blenheim.

Defoe's *The Review* began publication (1704–1713).

His love letters to the actress Elizabeth Barry, Rochester's mistress, published in *Familiar Letters: Written by the . . . Earl of Rochester, and Several Other Persons of Honor and Quality*.

Swift's *A Tale of a Tub* and *The Battle of the Books* published.

Cibber's *THE CARELESS HUS-BAND.*

1705

Haymarket Theatre opened.

Steele's *THE TENDER HUS-BAND.*

1706

Battle of Ramillies.

Farquhar's *THE RECRUITING OFFICER.*

1707

Union of Scotland and England.

Death of Farquhar.

Henry Fielding born.

Farquhar's *THE BEAUX' STRAT-AGEM.*

1708

Downes' *Roscius Anglicanus* published.

1709

Samuel Johnson born.

Rowe's edition of Shakespeare published.

The Tatler began publication (1709–1711)

Centlivre's *THE BUSY BODY.*

1711

Shaftesbury's *Characteristics* published.

The Spectator began publication (1711–1712).

Pope's *An Essay on Criticism* published.

1713

Treaty of Utrecht ended the War of the Spanish Succession.

Addison's *CATO.*

1714

Death of Anne; accession of George I.

Steele became Governor of Drury Lane.
John Rich assumed management of Lincoln's Inn Fields.
Centlivre's *THE WONDER: A WOMAN KEEPS A SECRET.*
Rowe's *JANE SHORE.*

1715
Jacobite Rebellion.
Death of Tate.
Rowe made Poet Laureate.
Death of Wycherley.

1716
Addison's *THE DRUMMER.*

1717
David Garrick born.
Cibber's *THE NON-JUROR.*
Gay, Pope, and Arbuthnot's *THREE HOURS AFTER MAR-RIAGE.*

1718
Death of Rowe.
Centlivre's *A BOLD STROKE FOR A WIFE.*

1719
Death of Addison.
Defoe's *Robinson Crusoe* published.
Young's *BUSIRIS, KING OF EGYPT.*

1720
South Sea Bubble.
Samuel Foote born.
Steele suspended from the Governorship of Drury Lane (restored 1721).
Little Theatre in the Haymarket opened.
Steele's *The Theatre* (periodical) published.
Hughes' *THE SIEGE OF DA-MASCUS.*

1721
Walpole became first Minister.

1722
Steele's *THE CONSCIOUS LOVERS.*

1723
Death of Susannah Centlivre.
Death of D'Urfey.

1725
Pope's edition of Shakespeare published.

1726
Death of Jeremy Collier.
Death of Vanbrugh.
Law's *Unlawfulness of Stage Entertainments* published.
Swift's *Gulliver's Travels* published.

1727
Death of George I; accession of George II.
Death of Sir Isaac Newton.
Arthur Murphy born.

1728
Pope's *The Dunciad* (first version) published.
Cibber's *THE PROVOKED HUSBAND* (expansion of Vanbrugh's fragment *A JOURNEY TO LONDON*).
Gay's *THE BEGGAR'S OPERA.*

1729
Goodman's Fields Theatre opened.
Death of Congreve.
Death of Steele.
Edmund Burke born.

1730
Cibber made Poet Laureate.
Oliver Goldsmith born.
Thomson's *The Seasons* published.
Fielding's *THE AUTHOR'S FARCE.*

Fielding's *TOM THUMB* (revised as *THE TRAGEDY OF TRAGE-DIES*, 1731).

1731

Death of Defoe.

Fielding's *THE GRUB-STREET OPERA*.

Lillo's *THE LONDON MERCH-ANT*.

1732

Covent Garden Theatre opened.

Death of Gay.

George Colman the elder born.

Fielding's *THE COVENT GARDEN TRAGEDY*.

Fielding's *THE MODERN HUS-BAND*.

Charles Johnson's *CAELIA*.

1733

Pope's *An Essay on Man* (Epistles I–III) published (Epistle IV, 1734).

1734

Death of Dennis.

The Prompter began publication (1734–1736).

Theobald's edition of Shakespeare published.

Fielding's *DON QUIXOTE IN ENGLAND*.

1736

Fielding led the "Great Mogul's Company of Comedians" at the Little Theatre in the Haymarket (1736–1737).

Fielding's *PASQUIN*.

Lillo's *FATAL CURIOSITY*.

1737

The Stage Licensing Act.

Dodsley's *THE KING AND THE MILLER OF MANSFIELD*.

Fielding's *THE HISTORICAL REGISTER FOR 1736*.